ISBN 0-8373-0089-4

C-89   CAREER EXAMINATION SERIES

This is your
PASSBOOK® for...

Bookkeeper

Test Preparation Study Guide

Questions & Answers

NATIONAL LEARNING CORPORATION

PASSBOOK SERIES®

THE *PASSBOOK SERIES®* has been created to prepare applicants and candidates for the ultimate academic battlefield – the examination room.

At some time in our lives, each and every one of us may be required to take an examination – for validation, matriculation, admission, qualification, registration, certification, or licensure.

Based on the assumption that every applicant or candidate has met the basic formal educational standards, has taken the required number of courses, and read the necessary texts, the *PASSBOOK SERIES®* furnishes the one special preparation which may assure passing with confidence, instead of failing with insecurity. Examination questions – together with answers – are furnished as the basic vehicle for study so that the mysteries of the examination and its compounding difficulties may be eliminated or diminished by a sure method.

This book is meant to help you pass your examination provided that you qualify and are serious in your objective.

The entire field is reviewed through the huge store of content information which is succinctly presented through a provocative and challenging approach – the question-and-answer method.

A climate of success is established by furnishing the correct answers at the end of each test.

You soon learn to recognize types of questions, forms of questions, and patterns of questioning. You may even begin to anticipate expected outcomes.

You perceive that many questions are repeated or adapted so that you can gain acute insights, which may enable you to score many sure points.

You learn how to confront new questions, or types of questions, and to attack them confidently and work out the correct answers.

You note objectives and emphases, and recognize pitfalls and dangers, so that you may make positive educational adjustments.

Moreover, you are kept fully informed in relation to new concepts, methods, practices, and directions in the field.

You discover that you are actually taking the examination all the time: you are preparing for the examination by "taking" an examination, not by reading extraneous and/or supererogatory textbooks.

In short, this PASSBOOK®, used directedly, should be an important factor in helping you to pass your test.

BOOKKEEPER

JOB DESCRIPTION

Under supervision, with little or some latitude for independent or unreviewed action, performs computations of varying degrees of difficulty and responsibility related to financial records. Performs all related work.

EXAMPLES OF TYPICAL TASKS

Performs computations and posts or compiles financial data as directed for accounting purposes, or for calculating balances, loans, or refunds; posts to general ledgers and journals; balances or adjusts accounts; assists in examining invoices, claims, vouchers, payrolls, fee collection reports or applications for allowances, loans, transfers and refunds and verifies their accuracy by consulting supporting financial records and data; prepares purchase orders, statements or bills; processes cash receipts; performs bank reconciliations; keeps records and makes reports as required; may deal with petty cash or imprest funds; may prepare required forms to enter data into a computerized system; may utilize manual and automated office systems.

TEST

The written test will be of the multiple-choice type and may include questions on examining and preparing payment and revenue documentation; classifying accounting transactions; maintaining accounts; reconciling accounts; analyzing accounting data; closing accounts; preparing reports and forms; and other related areas.

———

HOW TO TAKE A TEST

I. YOU MUST PASS AN EXAMINATION

A. *WHAT EVERY CANDIDATE SHOULD KNOW*

Examination applicants often ask us for help in preparing for the written test. What can I study in advance? What kinds of questions will be asked? How will the test be given? How will the papers be graded?

As an applicant for a civil service examination, you may be wondering about some of these things. Our purpose here is to suggest effective methods of advance study and to describe civil service examinations.

Your chances for success on this examination can be increased if you know how to prepare. Those "pre-examination jitters" can be reduced if you know what to expect. You can even experience an adventure in good citizenship if you know why civil service exams are given.

B. *WHY ARE CIVIL SERVICE EXAMINATIONS GIVEN?*

Civil service examinations are important to you in two ways. As a citizen, you want public jobs filled by employees who know how to do their work. As a job seeker, you want a fair chance to compete for that job on an equal footing with other candidates. The best-known means of accomplishing this two-fold goal is the competitive examination.

Exams are widely publicized throughout the nation. They may be administered for jobs in federal, state, city, municipal, town or village governments or agencies.

Any citizen may apply, with some limitations, such as the age or residence of applicants. Your experience and education may be reviewed to see whether you meet the requirements for the particular examination. When these requirements exist, they are reasonable and applied consistently to all applicants. Thus, a competitive examination may cause you some uneasiness now, but it is your privilege and safeguard.

C. *HOW ARE CIVIL SERVICE EXAMS DEVELOPED?*

Examinations are carefully written by trained technicians who are specialists in the field known as "psychological measurement," in consultation with recognized authorities in the field of work that the test will cover. These experts recommend the subject matter areas or skills to be tested; only those knowledges or skills important to your success on the job are included. The most reliable books and source materials available are used as references. Together, the experts and technicians judge the difficulty level of the questions.

Test technicians know how to phrase questions so that the problem is clearly stated. Their ethics do not permit "trick" or "catch" questions. Questions may have been tried out on sample groups, or subjected to statistical analysis, to determine their usefulness.

Written tests are often used in combination with performance tests, ratings of training and experience, and oral interviews. All of these measures combine to form the best-known means of finding the right person for the right job.

II. HOW TO PASS THE WRITTEN TEST

A. NATURE OF THE EXAMINATION

To prepare intelligently for civil service examinations, you should know how they differ from school examinations you have taken. In school you were assigned certain definite pages to read or subjects to cover. The examination questions were quite detailed and usually emphasized memory. Civil service exams, on the other hand, try to discover your present ability to perform the duties of a position, plus your potentiality to learn these duties. In other words, a civil service exam attempts to predict how successful you will be. Questions cover such a broad area that they cannot be as minute and detailed as school exam questions.

In the public service similar kinds of work, or positions, are grouped together in one "class." This process is known as *position-classification*. All the positions in a class are paid according to the salary range for that class. One class title covers all of these positions, and they are all tested by the same examination.

B. FOUR BASIC STEPS

1) Study the announcement

How, then, can you know what subjects to study? Our best answer is: "Learn as much as possible about the class of positions for which you've applied." The exam will test the knowledge, skills and abilities needed to do the work.

Your most valuable source of information about the position you want is the official exam announcement. This announcement lists the training and experience qualifications. Check these standards and apply only if you come reasonably close to meeting them.

The brief description of the position in the examination announcement offers some clues to the subjects which will be tested. Think about the job itself. Review the duties in your mind. Can you perform them, or are there some in which you are rusty? Fill in the blank spots in your preparation.

Many jurisdictions preview the written test in the exam announcement by including a section called "Knowledge and Abilities Required," "Scope of the Examination," or some similar heading. Here you will find out specifically what fields will be tested.

2) Review your own background

Once you learn in general what the position is all about, and what you need to know to do the work, ask yourself which subjects you already know fairly well and which need improvement. You may wonder whether to concentrate on improving your strong areas or on building some background in your fields of weakness. When the announcement has specified "some knowledge" or "considerable knowledge," or has used adjectives like "beginning principles of…" or "advanced … methods," you can get a clue as to the number and difficulty of questions to be asked in any given field. More questions, and hence broader coverage, would be included for those subjects which are more important in the work. Now weigh your strengths and weaknesses against the job requirements and prepare accordingly.

3) Determine the level of the position

Another way to tell how intensively you should prepare is to understand the level of the job for which you are applying. Is it the entering level? In other words, is this the position in which beginners in a field of work are hired? Or is it an intermediate or advanced level? Sometimes this is indicated by such words as "Junior" or "Senior" in the class title. Other jurisdictions use Roman numerals to designate the level – Clerk I, Clerk II, for example. The word "Supervisor" sometimes appears in the title. If the level is not indicated by the title, check the description of duties. Will you be working under very close supervision, or will you have responsibility for independent decisions in this work?

4) Choose appropriate study materials

Now that you know the subjects to be examined and the relative amount of each subject to be covered, you can choose suitable study materials. For beginning level jobs, or even advanced ones, if you have a pronounced weakness in some aspect of your training, read a modern, standard textbook in that field. Be sure it is up to date and has general coverage. Such books are normally available at your library, and the librarian will be glad to help you locate one. For entry-level positions, questions of appropriate difficulty are chosen – neither highly advanced questions, nor those too simple. Such questions require careful thought but not advanced training.

If the position for which you are applying is technical or advanced, you will read more advanced, specialized material. If you are already familiar with the basic principles of your field, elementary textbooks would waste your time. Concentrate on advanced textbooks and technical periodicals. Think through the concepts and review difficult problems in your field.

These are all general sources. You can get more ideas on your own initiative, following these leads. For example, training manuals and publications of the government agency which employs workers in your field can be useful, particularly for technical and professional positions. A letter or visit to the government department involved may result in more specific study suggestions, and certainly will provide you with a more definite idea of the exact nature of the position you are seeking.

III. KINDS OF TESTS

Tests are used for purposes other than measuring knowledge and ability to perform specified duties. For some positions, it is equally important to test ability to make adjustments to new situations or to profit from training. In others, basic mental abilities not dependent on information are essential. Questions which test these things may not appear as pertinent to the duties of the position as those which test for knowledge and information. Yet they are often highly important parts of a fair examination. For very general questions, it is almost impossible to help you direct your study efforts. What we can do is to point out some of the more common of these general abilities needed in public service positions and describe some typical questions.

1) General information

Broad, general information has been found useful for predicting job success in some kinds of work. This is tested in a variety of ways, from vocabulary lists to questions about current events. Basic background in some field of work, such as sociology or economics, may be sampled in a group of questions. Often these are principles which have become familiar to most persons through exposure rather than through formal training. It is difficult to advise you how to study for these questions; being alert to the world around you is our best suggestion.

2) Verbal ability

An example of an ability needed in many positions is verbal or language ability. Verbal ability is, in brief, the ability to use and understand words. Vocabulary and grammar tests are typical measures of this ability. Reading comprehension or paragraph interpretation questions are common in many kinds of civil service tests. You are given a paragraph of written material and asked to find its central meaning.

3) Numerical ability

Number skills can be tested by the familiar arithmetic problem, by checking paired lists of numbers to see which are alike and which are different, or by interpreting charts and graphs. In the latter test, a graph may be printed in the test booklet which you are asked to use as the basis for answering questions.

4) Observation

A popular test for law-enforcement positions is the observation test. A picture is shown to you for several minutes, then taken away. Questions about the picture test your ability to observe both details and larger elements.

5) Following directions

In many positions in the public service, the employee must be able to carry out written instructions dependably and accurately. You may be given a chart with several columns, each column listing a variety of information. The questions require you to carry out directions involving the information given in the chart.

6) Skills and aptitudes

Performance tests effectively measure some manual skills and aptitudes. When the skill is one in which you are trained, such as typing or shorthand, you can practice. These tests are often very much like those given in business school or high school courses. For many of the other skills and aptitudes, however, no short-time preparation can be made. Skills and abilities natural to you or that you have developed throughout your lifetime are being tested.

Many of the general questions just described provide all the data needed to answer the questions and ask you to use your reasoning ability to find the answers. Your best preparation for these tests, as well as for tests of facts and ideas, is to be at your physical and mental best. You, no doubt, have your own methods of getting into an exam-taking mood and keeping "in shape." The next section lists some ideas on this subject.

IV. KINDS OF QUESTIONS

Only rarely is the "essay" question, which you answer in narrative form, used in civil service tests. Civil service tests are usually of the short-answer type. Full instructions for answering these questions will be given to you at the examination. But in case this is your first experience with short-answer questions and separate answer sheets, here is what you need to know:

4

1) Multiple-choice Questions

Most popular of the short-answer questions is the "multiple choice" or "best answer" question. It can be used, for example, to test for factual knowledge, ability to solve problems or judgment in meeting situations found at work.

A multiple-choice question is normally one of three types—

- It can begin with an incomplete statement followed by several possible endings. You are to find the one ending which *best* completes the statement, although some of the others may not be entirely wrong.
- It can also be a complete statement in the form of a question which is answered by choosing one of the statements listed.
- It can be in the form of a problem – again you select the best answer.

Here is an example of a multiple-choice question with a discussion which should give you some clues as to the method for choosing the right answer:

When an employee has a complaint about his assignment, the action which will *best* help him overcome his difficulty is to
  A. discuss his difficulty with his coworkers
  B. take the problem to the head of the organization
  C. take the problem to the person who gave him the assignment
  D. say nothing to anyone about his complaint

In answering this question, you should study each of the choices to find which is best. Consider choice "A" – Certainly an employee may discuss his complaint with fellow employees, but no change or improvement can result, and the complaint remains unresolved. Choice "B" is a poor choice since the head of the organization probably does not know what assignment you have been given, and taking your problem to him is known as "going over the head" of the supervisor. The supervisor, or person who made the assignment, is the person who can clarify it or correct any injustice. Choice "C" is, therefore, correct. To say nothing, as in choice "D," is unwise. Supervisors have and interest in knowing the problems employees are facing, and the employee is seeking a solution to his problem.

2) True/False Questions

The "true/false" or "right/wrong" form of question is sometimes used. Here a complete statement is given. Your job is to decide whether the statement is right or wrong.

SAMPLE: A person-to-person long-distance telephone call costs less than a station-to-station call to the same city.

This statement is wrong, or false, since person-to-person calls are more expensive.

This is not a complete list of all possible question forms, although most of the others are variations of these common types. You will always get complete directions for answering questions. Be sure you understand *how* to mark your answers – ask questions until you do.

V. RECORDING YOUR ANSWERS

For an examination with very few applicants, you may be told to record your answers in the test booklet itself. Separate answer sheets are much more common. If this separate answer sheet is to be scored by machine – and this is often the case – it is highly important that you mark your answers correctly in order to get credit.

An electric scoring machine is often used in civil service offices because of the speed with which papers can be scored. Machine-scored answer sheets must be marked with a pencil, which will be given to you. This pencil has a high graphite content which responds to the electric scoring machine. As a matter of fact, stray dots may register as answers, so do not let your pencil rest on the answer sheet while you are pondering the correct answer. Also, if your pencil lead breaks or is otherwise defective, ask for another.

Since the answer sheet will be dropped in a slot in the scoring machine, be careful not to bend the corners or get the paper crumpled.

The answer sheet normally has five vertical columns of numbers, with 30 numbers to a column. These numbers correspond to the question numbers in your test booklet. After each number, going across the page are four or five pairs of dotted lines. These short dotted lines have small letters or numbers above them. The first two pairs may also have a "T" or "F" above the letters. This indicates that the first two pairs only are to be used if the questions are of the true-false type. If the questions are multiple choice, disregard the "T" and "F" and pay attention only to the small letters or numbers.

Answer your questions in the manner of the sample that follows:

32. The largest city in the United States is
    A. Washington, D.C.
    B. New York City
    C. Chicago
    D. Detroit
    E. San Francisco

1) Choose the answer you think is best. (New York City is the largest, so "B" is correct.)
2) Find the row of dotted lines numbered the same as the question you are answering. (Find row number 32)
3) Find the pair of dotted lines corresponding to the answer. (Find the pair of lines under the mark "B.")
4) Make a solid black mark between the dotted lines.

VI. BEFORE THE TEST

Common sense will help you find procedures to follow to get ready for an examination. Too many of us, however, overlook these sensible measures. Indeed, nervousness and fatigue have been found to be the most serious reasons why applicants fail to do their best on civil service tests. Here is a list of reminders:

- Begin your preparation early – Don't wait until the last minute to go scurrying around for books and materials or to find out what the position is all about.
- Prepare continuously – An hour a night for a week is better than an all-night cram session. This has been definitely established. What is more, a night a

week for a month will return better dividends than crowding your study into a shorter period of time.

- Locate the place of the exam – You have been sent a notice telling you when and where to report for the examination. If the location is in a different town or otherwise unfamiliar to you, it would be well to inquire the best route and learn something about the building.
- Relax the night before the test – Allow your mind to rest. Do not study at all that night. Plan some mild recreation or diversion; then go to bed early and get a good night's sleep.
- Get up early enough to make a leisurely trip to the place for the test – This way unforeseen events, traffic snarls, unfamiliar buildings, etc. will not upset you.
- Dress comfortably – A written test is not a fashion show. You will be known by number and not by name, so wear something comfortable.
- Leave excess paraphernalia at home – Shopping bags and odd bundles will get in your way. You need bring only the items mentioned in the official notice you received; usually everything you need is provided. Do not bring reference books to the exam. They will only confuse those last minutes and be taken away from you when in the test room.
- Arrive somewhat ahead of time – If because of transportation schedules you must get there very early, bring a newspaper or magazine to take your mind off yourself while waiting.
- Locate the examination room – When you have found the proper room, you will be directed to the seat or part of the room where you will sit. Sometimes you are given a sheet of instructions to read while you are waiting. Do not fill out any forms until you are told to do so; just read them and be prepared.
- Relax and prepare to listen to the instructions
- If you have any physical problem that may keep you from doing your best, be sure to tell the test administrator. If you are sick or in poor health, you really cannot do your best on the exam. You can come back and take the test some other time.

VII. AT THE TEST

The day of the test is here and you have the test booklet in your hand. The temptation to get going is very strong. Caution! There is more to success than knowing the right answers. You must know how to identify your papers and understand variations in the type of short-answer question used in this particular examination. Follow these suggestions for maximum results from your efforts:

1) Cooperate with the monitor

The test administrator has a duty to create a situation in which you can be as much at ease as possible. He will give instructions, tell you when to begin, check to see that you are marking your answer sheet correctly, and so on. He is not there to guard you, although he will see that your competitors do not take unfair advantage. He wants to help you do your best.

2) Listen to all instructions

Don't jump the gun! Wait until you understand all directions. In most civil service tests you get more time than you need to answer the questions. So don't be in a hurry.

Read each word of instructions until you clearly understand the meaning. Study the examples, listen to all announcements and follow directions. Ask questions if you do not understand what to do.

3) Identify your papers

Civil service exams are usually identified by number only. You will be assigned a number; you must not put your name on your test papers. Be sure to copy your number correctly. Since more than one exam may be given, copy your exact examination title.

4) Plan your time

Unless you are told that a test is a "speed" or "rate of work" test, speed itself is usually not important. Time enough to answer all the questions will be provided, but this does not mean that you have all day. An overall time limit has been set. Divide the total time (in minutes) by the number of questions to determine the approximate time you have for each question.

5) Do not linger over difficult questions

If you come across a difficult question, mark it with a paper clip (useful to have along) and come back to it when you have been through the booklet. One caution if you do this – be sure to skip a number on your answer sheet as well. Check often to be sure that you have not lost your place and that you are marking in the row numbered the same as the question you are answering.

6) Read the questions

Be sure you know what the question asks! Many capable people are unsuccessful because they failed to *read* the questions correctly.

7) Answer all questions

Unless you have been instructed that a penalty will be deducted for incorrect answers, it is better to guess than to omit a question.

8) Speed tests

It is often better NOT to guess on speed tests. It has been found that on timed tests people are tempted to spend the last few seconds before time is called in marking answers at random – without even reading them – in the hope of picking up a few extra points. To discourage this practice, the instructions may warn you that your score will be "corrected" for guessing. That is, a penalty will be applied. The incorrect answers will be deducted from the correct ones, or some other penalty formula will be used.

9) Review your answers

If you finish before time is called, go back to the questions you guessed or omitted to give them further thought. Review other answers if you have time.

10) Return your test materials

If you are ready to leave before others have finished or time is called, take ALL your materials to the monitor and leave quietly. Never take any test material with you. The monitor can discover whose papers are not complete, and taking a test booklet may be grounds for disqualification.

VIII. EXAMINATION TECHNIQUES

1) Read the general instructions carefully. These are usually printed on the first page of the exam booklet. As a rule, these instructions refer to the timing of the examination; the fact that you should not start work until the signal and must stop work at a signal, etc. If there are any *special* instructions, such as a choice of questions to be answered, make sure that you note this instruction carefully.

2) When you are ready to start work on the examination, that is as soon as the signal has been given, read the instructions to each question booklet, underline any key words or phrases, such as *least, best, outline, describe* and the like. In this way you will tend to answer as requested rather than discover on reviewing your paper that you *listed without describing*, that you selected the *worst* choice rather than the *best* choice, etc.

3) If the examination is of the objective or multiple-choice type – that is, each question will also give a series of possible answers: A, B, C or D, and you are called upon to select the best answer and write the letter next to that answer on your answer paper – it is advisable to start answering each question in turn. There may be anywhere from 50 to 100 such questions in the three or four hours allotted and you can see how much time would be taken if you read through all the questions before beginning to answer any. Furthermore, if you come across a question or group of questions which you know would be difficult to answer, it would undoubtedly affect your handling of all the other questions.

4) If the examination is of the essay type and contains but a few questions, it is a moot point as to whether you should read all the questions before starting to answer any one. Of course, if you are given a choice – say five out of seven and the like – then it is essential to read all the questions so you can eliminate the two that are most difficult. If, however, you are asked to answer all the questions, there may be danger in trying to answer the easiest one first because you may find that you will spend too much time on it. The best technique is to answer the first question, then proceed to the second, etc.

5) Time your answers. Before the exam begins, write down the time it started, then add the time allowed for the examination and write down the time it must be completed, then divide the time available somewhat as follows:
   - If 3-1/2 hours are allowed, that would be 210 minutes. If you have 80 objective-type questions, that would be an average of 2-1/2 minutes per question. Allow yourself no more than 2 minutes per question, or a total of 160 minutes, which will permit about 50 minutes to review.
   - If for the time allotment of 210 minutes there are 7 essay questions to answer, that would average about 30 minutes a question. Give yourself only 25 minutes per question so that you have about 35 minutes to review.

6) The most important instruction is to *read each question* and make sure you know what is wanted. The second most important instruction is to *time yourself properly* so that you answer every question. The third most

important instruction is to *answer every question*. Guess if you have to but include something for each question. Remember that you will receive no credit for a blank and will probably receive some credit if you write something in answer to an essay question. If you guess a letter – say "B" for a multiple-choice question – you may have guessed right. If you leave a blank as an answer to a multiple-choice question, the examiners may respect your feelings but it will not add a point to your score. Some exams may penalize you for wrong answers, so in such cases *only*, you may not want to guess unless you have some basis for your answer.

7) Suggestions
   a. Objective-type questions
      1. Examine the question booklet for proper sequence of pages and questions
      2. Read all instructions carefully
      3. Skip any question which seems too difficult; return to it after all other questions have been answered
      4. Apportion your time properly; do not spend too much time on any single question or group of questions
      5. Note and underline key words – *all, most, fewest, least, best, worst, same, opposite,* etc.
      6. Pay particular attention to negatives
      7. Note unusual option, e.g., unduly long, short, complex, different or similar in content to the body of the question
      8. Observe the use of "hedging" words – *probably, may, most likely,* etc.
      9. Make sure that your answer is put next to the same number as the question
      10. Do not second-guess unless you have good reason to believe the second answer is definitely more correct
      11. Cross out original answer if you decide another answer is more accurate; do not erase until you are ready to hand your paper in
      12. Answer all questions; guess unless instructed otherwise
      13. Leave time for review

   b. Essay questions
      1. Read each question carefully
      2. Determine exactly what is wanted. Underline key words or phrases.
      3. Decide on outline or paragraph answer
      4. Include many different points and elements unless asked to develop any one or two points or elements
      5. Show impartiality by giving pros and cons unless directed to select one side only
      6. Make and write down any assumptions you find necessary to answer the questions
      7. Watch your English, grammar, punctuation and choice of words
      8. Time your answers; don't crowd material

8) Answering the essay question

Most essay questions can be answered by framing the specific response around several key words or ideas. Here are a few such key words or ideas:

M's: manpower, materials, methods, money, management
P's: purpose, program, policy, plan, procedure, practice, problems, pitfalls, personnel, public relations

    a. Six basic steps in handling problems:
1. Preliminary plan and background development
2. Collect information, data and facts
3. Analyze and interpret information, data and facts
4. Analyze and develop solutions as well as make recommendations
5. Prepare report and sell recommendations
6. Install recommendations and follow up effectiveness

    b. Pitfalls to avoid
1. *Taking things for granted* – A statement of the situation does not necessarily imply that each of the elements is necessarily true; for example, a complaint may be invalid and biased so that all that can be taken for granted is that a complaint has been registered
2. *Considering only one side of a situation* – Wherever possible, indicate several alternatives and then point out the reasons you selected the best one
3. *Failing to indicate follow up* – Whenever your answer indicates action on your part, make certain that you will take proper follow-up action to see how successful your recommendations, procedures or actions turn out to be
4. *Taking too long in answering any single question* – Remember to time your answers properly

IX. AFTER THE TEST

Scoring procedures differ in detail among civil service jurisdictions although the general principles are the same. Whether the papers are hand-scored or graded by machine we have described, they are nearly always graded by number. That is, the person who marks the paper knows only the number – never the name – of the applicant. Not until all the papers have been graded will they be matched with names. If other tests, such as training and experience or oral interview ratings have been given, scores will be combined. Different parts of the examination usually have different weights. For example, the written test might count 60 percent of the final grade, and a rating of training and experience 40 percent. In many jurisdictions, veterans will have a certain number of points added to their grades.

After the final grade has been determined, the names are placed in grade order and an eligible list is established. There are various methods for resolving ties between those who get the same final grade – probably the most common is to place first the name of the person whose application was received first. Job offers are made from the eligible list in the order the names appear on it. You will be notified of your grade and your rank as soon as all these computations have been made. This will be done as rapidly as possible.

People who are found to meet the requirements in the announcement are called "eligibles." Their names are put on a list of eligible candidates. An eligible's chances of getting a job depend on how high he stands on this list and how fast agencies are filling jobs from the list.

When a job is to be filled from a list of eligibles, the agency asks for the names of people on the list of eligibles for that job. When the civil service commission receives this request, it sends to the agency the names of the three people highest on this list. Or, if the job to be filled has specialized requirements, the office sends the agency the names of the top three persons who meet these requirements from the general list.

The appointing officer makes a choice from among the three people whose names were sent to him. If the selected person accepts the appointment, the names of the others are put back on the list to be considered for future openings.

That is the rule in hiring from all kinds of eligible lists, whether they are for typist, carpenter, chemist, or something else. For every vacancy, the appointing officer has his choice of any one of the top three eligibles on the list. This explains why the person whose name is on top of the list sometimes does not get an appointment when some of the persons lower on the list do. If the appointing officer chooses the second or third eligible, the No. 1 eligible does not get a job at once, but stays on the list until he is appointed or the list is terminated.

X. HOW TO PASS THE INTERVIEW TEST

The examination for which you applied requires an oral interview test. You have already taken the written test and you are now being called for the interview test – the final part of the formal examination.

You may think that it is not possible to prepare for an interview test and that there are no procedures to follow during an interview. Our purpose is to point out some things you can do in advance that will help you and some good rules to follow and pitfalls to avoid while you are being interviewed.

What is an interview supposed to test?

The written examination is designed to test the technical knowledge and competence of the candidate; the oral is designed to evaluate intangible qualities, not readily measured otherwise, and to establish a list showing the relative fitness of each candidate – as measured against his competitors – for the position sought. Scoring is not on the basis of "right" and "wrong," but on a sliding scale of values ranging from "not passable" to "outstanding." As a matter of fact, it is possible to achieve a relatively low score without a single "incorrect" answer because of evident weakness in the qualities being measured.

Occasionally, an examination may consist entirely of an oral test – either an individual or a group oral. In such cases, information is sought concerning the technical knowledges and abilities of the candidate, since there has been no written examination for this purpose. More commonly, however, an oral test is used to supplement a written examination.

Who conducts interviews?

The composition of oral boards varies among different jurisdictions. In nearly all, a representative of the personnel department serves as chairman. One of the members of the board may be a representative of the department in which the candidate would work. In some cases, "outside experts" are used, and, frequently, a businessman or some other representative of the general public is asked to serve. Labor and management or other special groups may be represented. The aim is to secure the services of experts in the appropriate field.

However the board is composed, it is a good idea (and not at all improper or unethical) to ascertain in advance of the interview who the members are and what groups they represent. When you are introduced to them, you will have some idea of their backgrounds and interests, and at least you will not stutter and stammer over their names.

What should be done before the interview?

While knowledge about the board members is useful and takes some of the surprise element out of the interview, there is other preparation which is more substantive. It *is* possible to prepare for an oral interview – in several ways:

1) Keep a copy of your application and review it carefully before the interview

This may be the only document before the oral board, and the starting point of the interview. Know what education and experience you have listed there, and the sequence and dates of all of it. Sometimes the board will ask you to review the highlights of your experience for them; you should not have to hem and haw doing it.

2) Study the class specification and the examination announcement

Usually, the oral board has one or both of these to guide them. The qualities, characteristics or knowledges required by the position sought are stated in these documents. They offer valuable clues as to the nature of the oral interview. For example, if the job involves supervisory responsibilities, the announcement will usually indicate that knowledge of modern supervisory methods and the qualifications of the candidate as a supervisor will be tested. If so, you can expect such questions, frequently in the form of a hypothetical situation which you are expected to solve. NEVER go into an oral without knowledge of the duties and responsibilities of the job you seek.

3) Think through each qualification required

Try to visualize the kind of questions you would ask if you were a board member. How well could you answer them? Try especially to appraise your own knowledge and background in each area, *measured against the job sought*, and identify any areas in which you are weak. Be critical and realistic – do not flatter yourself.

4) Do some general reading in areas in which you feel you may be weak

For example, if the job involves supervision and your past experience has NOT, some general reading in supervisory methods and practices, particularly in the field of human relations, might be useful. Do NOT study agency procedures or detailed manuals. The oral board will be testing your understanding and capacity, not your memory.

5) Get a good night's sleep and watch your general health and mental attitude

You will want a clear head at the interview. Take care of a cold or any other minor ailment, and of course, no hangovers.

What should be done on the day of the interview?

Now comes the day of the interview itself. Give yourself plenty of time to get there. Plan to arrive somewhat ahead of the scheduled time, particularly if your appointment is in the fore part of the day. If a previous candidate fails to appear, the board might be ready for you a bit early. By early afternoon an oral board is almost invariably behind schedule if there are many candidates, and you may have to wait.

Take along a book or magazine to read, or your application to review, but leave any extraneous material in the waiting room when you go in for your interview. In any event, relax and compose yourself.

The matter of dress is important. The board is forming impressions about you – from your experience, your manners, your attitude, and your appearance. Give your personal appearance careful attention. Dress your best, but not your flashiest. Choose conservative, appropriate clothing, and be sure it is immaculate. This is a business interview, and your appearance should indicate that you regard it as such. Besides, being well groomed and properly dressed will help boost your confidence.

Sooner or later, someone will call your name and escort you into the interview room. *This is it.* From here on you are on your own. It is too late for any more preparation. But remember, you asked for this opportunity to prove your fitness, and you are here because your request was granted.

What happens when you go in?

The usual sequence of events will be as follows: The clerk (who is often the board stenographer) will introduce you to the chairman of the oral board, who will introduce you to the other members of the board. Acknowledge the introductions before you sit down. Do not be surprised if you find a microphone facing you or a stenotypist sitting by. Oral interviews are usually recorded in the event of an appeal or other review.

Usually the chairman of the board will open the interview by reviewing the highlights of your education and work experience from your application – primarily for the benefit of the other members of the board, as well as to get the material into the record. Do not interrupt or comment unless there is an error or significant misinterpretation; if that is the case, do not hesitate. But do not quibble about insignificant matters. Also, he will usually ask you some question about your education, experience or your present job – partly to get you to start talking and to establish the interviewing "rapport." He may start the actual questioning, or turn it over to one of the other members. Frequently, each member undertakes the questioning on a particular area, one in which he is perhaps most competent, so you can expect each member to participate in the examination. Because time is limited, you may also expect some rather abrupt switches in the direction the questioning takes, so do not be upset by it. Normally, a board member will not pursue a single line of questioning unless he discovers a particular strength or weakness.

After each member has participated, the chairman will usually ask whether any member has any further questions, then will ask you if you have anything you wish to add. Unless you are expecting this question, it may floor you. Worse, it may start you off on an extended, extemporaneous speech. The board is not usually seeking more information. The question is principally to offer you a last opportunity to present further qualifications or to indicate that you have nothing to add. So, if you feel that a significant qualification or characteristic has been overlooked, it is proper to point it out in a sentence or so. Do not compliment the board on the thoroughness of their examination – they have been sketchy, and you know it. If you wish, merely say, "No thank you, I have nothing further to add." This is a point where you can "talk yourself out" of a good impression or fail to present an important bit of information. Remember, *you close the interview yourself.*

The chairman will then say, "That is all, Mr. _____, thank you." Do not be startled; the interview is over, and quicker than you think. Thank him, gather your belongings and take your leave. Save your sigh of relief for the other side of the door.

How to put your best foot forward

Throughout this entire process, you may feel that the board individually and collectively is trying to pierce your defenses, seek out your hidden weaknesses and embarrass and confuse you. Actually, this is not true. They are obliged to make an appraisal of your qualifications for the job you are seeking, and they want to see you in your best light. Remember, they must interview all candidates and a non-cooperative candidate may become a failure in spite of their best efforts to bring out his qualifications. Here are 15 suggestions that will help you:

1) Be natural – Keep your attitude confident, not cocky

If you are not confident that you can do the job, do not expect the board to be. Do not apologize for your weaknesses, try to bring out your strong points. The board is interested in a positive, not negative, presentation. Cockiness will antagonize any board member and make him wonder if you are covering up a weakness by a false show of strength.

2) Get comfortable, but don't lounge or sprawl

Sit erectly but not stiffly. A careless posture may lead the board to conclude that you are careless in other things, or at least that you are not impressed by the importance of the occasion. Either conclusion is natural, even if incorrect. Do not fuss with your clothing, a pencil or an ashtray. Your hands may occasionally be useful to emphasize a point; do not let them become a point of distraction.

3) Do not wisecrack or make small talk

This is a serious situation, and your attitude should show that you consider it as such. Further, the time of the board is limited – they do not want to waste it, and neither should you.

4) Do not exaggerate your experience or abilities

In the first place, from information in the application or other interviews and sources, the board may know more about you than you think. Secondly, you probably will not get away with it. An experienced board is rather adept at spotting such a situation, so do not take the chance.

5) If you know a board member, do not make a point of it, yet do not hide it

Certainly you are not fooling him, and probably not the other members of the board. Do not try to take advantage of your acquaintanceship – it will probably do you little good.

6) Do not dominate the interview

Let the board do that. They will give you the clues – do not assume that you have to do all the talking. Realize that the board has a number of questions to ask you, and do not try to take up all the interview time by showing off your extensive knowledge of the answer to the first one.

7) Be attentive

You only have 20 minutes or so, and you should keep your attention at its sharpest throughout. When a member is addressing a problem or question to you, give him your undivided attention. Address your reply principally to him, but do not exclude the other board members.

8) Do not interrupt

A board member may be stating a problem for you to analyze. He will ask you a question when the time comes. Let him state the problem, and wait for the question.

9) Make sure you understand the question

Do not try to answer until you are sure what the question is. If it is not clear, restate it in your own words or ask the board member to clarify it for you. However, do not haggle about minor elements.

10) Reply promptly but not hastily

A common entry on oral board rating sheets is "candidate responded readily," or "candidate hesitated in replies." Respond as promptly and quickly as you can, but do not jump to a hasty, ill-considered answer.

11) Do not be peremptory in your answers

A brief answer is proper – but do not fire your answer back. That is a losing game from your point of view. The board member can probably ask questions much faster than you can answer them.

12) Do not try to create the answer you think the board member wants

He is interested in what kind of mind you have and how it works – not in playing games. Furthermore, he can usually spot this practice and will actually grade you down on it.

13) Do not switch sides in your reply merely to agree with a board member

Frequently, a member will take a contrary position merely to draw you out and to see if you are willing and able to defend your point of view. Do not start a debate, yet do not surrender a good position. If a position is worth taking, it is worth defending.

14) Do not be afraid to admit an error in judgment if you are shown to be wrong

The board knows that you are forced to reply without any opportunity for careful consideration. Your answer may be demonstrably wrong. If so, admit it and get on with the interview.

15) Do not dwell at length on your present job

The opening question may relate to your present assignment. Answer the question but do not go into an extended discussion. You are being examined for a *new* job, not your present one. As a matter of fact, try to phrase ALL your answers in terms of the job for which you are being examined.

Basis of Rating

Probably you will forget most of these "do's" and "don'ts" when you walk into the oral interview room. Even remembering them all will not ensure you a passing grade. Perhaps you did not have the qualifications in the first place. But remembering them will help you to put your best foot forward, without treading on the toes of the board members.

Rumor and popular opinion to the contrary notwithstanding, an oral board wants you to make the best appearance possible. They know you are under pressure – but they also want to see how you respond to it as a guide to what your reaction would be under the pressures of the job you seek. They will be influenced by the degree of poise you display, the personal traits you show and the manner in which you respond.

EXAMINATION SECTION

EXAMINATION SECTION
TEST 1

DIRECTIONS: Each question or incomplete statement is followed by several suggested answers or completions. Select the one that BEST answers the question or completes the statement. *PRINT THE LETTER OF THE CORRECT ANSWER IN THE SPACE AT THE RIGHT.*

1. In the preparation of a balance sheet, failure to consider the inventory of office supplies will result in _____ assets and _____.

    A. overstating; overstating liabilities
    B. understating; overstating capital
    C. understating; understating capital
    D. overstating; understating liabilities

1._____

2. The annual federal unemployment tax is paid by the

    A. employer *only*
    B. employee *only*
    C. employer and the employee equally
    D. employee, up to a maximum of 30 cents per week, and the balance is paid by the employer

2._____

3. Which are NORMALLY considered as current assets?

    A. Bank overdrafts
    B. Prepaid expenses
    C. Accrued expenses
    D. Payroll taxes

3._____

4. What type of ledger account is a summary of a number of accounts in another ledger? The _____ account.

    A. controlling
    B. subsidiary
    C. asset
    D. proprietorship

4._____

5. The PRIMARY purpose of a petty cash fund is to

    A. provide a fund for paying all miscellaneous expenses
    B. take the place of the cash account
    C. provide a common drawing fund for the owners of the business
    D. avoid entering a number of small amounts in the Cash Payments Journal

5._____

6. In the absence of a written agreement, profits in a partnership would be divided

    A. in proportion to the investment of the partners
    B. on an equitable basis depending on the time and effort spent by the partners
    C. equally
    D. on a ratio of investment basis, giving the senior partner preference

6._____

7. Which account represents a subtraction or decrease to an income account?

    A. Purchase Returns & Allowances
    B. Sales Returns & Allowances
    C. Freight In
    D. Prepaid Rent

7._____

8. If the Interest Expense account showed a debit balance of $210 as of December 31, and $40 of this amount was prepaid on Notes Payable, which statement is CORRECT as of December 31?

    A. Prepaid Interest of $170 should be shown as a deferred expense in the balance sheet.
    B. Interest Expense should be shown in the Income Statement as $210.
    C. Prepaid Interest of $40 should be listed as a deferred credit to income in the balance sheet.
    D. Interest Expense should be shown in the Income Statement as $170.

8.____

9. When prices are rising, which inventory-valuation method results in the LOWEST inventory value?

    A. FIFO   B. LIFO
    C. Average cost   D. Declining balance

9.____

10. Which of the following is a CORRECT procedure in preparing a bank reconciliation?

    A. Deposits in transit should be added to the cash balance on the books, and outstanding checks should be deducted from the cash balance on the bank statement.
    B. The cash balance on the bank statement and the cash balance on the books should be equal if there are deposits in transit and outstanding checks.
    C. Outstanding checks should be deducted from the cash balance on the books.
    D. Any service charge should be deducted from the check stub balance.

10.____

11. Which ratio indicates that there may NOT be enough on hand to meet current obligations?

    A. $\dfrac{\text{fixed assets}}{\text{fixed liabilities}} = \dfrac{2}{3}$ B. $\dfrac{\text{total assets}}{\text{total obligations}} = \dfrac{3}{5}$

    C. $\dfrac{\text{current assets}}{\text{current liabilities}} = \dfrac{1}{3}$ D. $\dfrac{\text{current assets}}{\text{fixed liabilities}} = \dfrac{1}{2}$

11.____

12. Which asset is NOT subject to depreciation?

    A. Factory equipment   B. Land
    C. Buildings   D. Machinery

12.____

13. Which form is prepared to verify that the total of the account balances in the Customers Ledger agrees with the balance in the controlling account in the General Ledger?

    A. Worksheet
    B. Schedule of accounts payable
    C. Schedule of accounts receivable
    D. Trial balance

13.____

14. If the merchandise inventory on hand at the end of the year was overstated, what will be the result of this error?   14.____

    A. *Understatement* of income for the year
    B. *Overstatement* of income for the year
    C. *Understatement* of assets at the end of the year
    D. No effect on income or assets

15. Working capital is found by subtracting the total current liabilities from the total   15.____

    A. fixed liabilities   B. fixed assets
    C. current income   D. current assets

16. Which is the CORRECT procedure for calculating the rate of merchandise turnover?   16.____

    A. Gross Sales divided by Net Sales
    B. Cost of Sales divided by Average Inventory
    C. Net Purchases divided by Average Inventory
    D. Gross Purchases divided by Net Purchases

17. The books of the Atlas Cement Corporation show a net profit of $142,000.   17.____
To close the Profit and Loss account of the corporation at the end of the year, the account CREDITED should be

    A. Earned Surplus   B. Capital Stock
    C. C. Atlas, Capital   D. C. Atlas, Personal

18. The bank statement at the end of the month indicated a bank charge for printing a new checkbook.   18.____
How is this information recorded?
Debit

    A. Cash and credit Office Supplies
    B. Office Supplies and credit the Bank Charges
    C. the Bank Charges and credit Office Supplies
    D. Miscellaneous Expense and credit Cash

19. The Allowance for Doubtful Accounts appears on the balance sheet as a deduction from   19.____

    A. Accounts Receivable   B. Notes Receivable
    C. Accounts Payable   D. Notes Payable

20. The Tucker Equipment Corporation had a $45,000 profit for the year ended December 31.   20.____
Which would be the PROPER entry to close the Income and Expense account at the end of the year?
Debit Income and Expense Summary; credit

    A. Tucker, Capital   B. Tucker, Drawing
    C. Retained Earnings   D. Capital Stock

21. A failure to record a purchases invoice would be discovered when the

    A.   monthly statement of account is sent to the customer
    B.   check is received from the customer
    C.   check is sent to the creditor
    D.   statement of account is received from the creditor

21.___

22. Which General Ledger account would appear in a post-closing trial balance?

    A.   Notes Receivable   B.   Bad Debts Expense
    C.   Sales Discount   D.   Fee Income

22.___

23. Which deduction is affected by the number of exemptions claimed?

    A.   State Disability   B.   State income tax
    C.   FICA tax   D.   Workers' Compensation

23.___

24. The face value of a 60-day, 12% promissory note is $900.
The maturity value of this note will be

    A. $909   B. $900   C. $918   D. $1,008

24.___

25. An invoice dated March 10, terms 2/10, n/30, should be paid no later than

    A.   March 20   B.   March 31   C.   April 9   D.   April 10

25.___

KEY (CORRECT ANSWERS)

1.	C		11.	C
2.	A		12.	B
3.	B		13.	C
4.	A		14.	B
5.	D		15.	D
6.	C		16.	B
7.	B		17.	A
8.	D		18.	D
9.	B		19.	A
10.	D		20.	C

21.	D
22.	A
23.	B
24.	C
25.	C

TEST 2

DIRECTIONS: Each question or incomplete statement is followed by several suggested answers or completions. Select the one that BEST answers the question or completes the statement. *PRINT THE LETTER OF THE CORRECT ANSWER IN THE SPACE AT THE RIGHT.*

1. Which is NOT an essential element of a computer system?　　　　　　　　　　　1.____

    A. Input   B. Central processing unit
    C. Verifier   D. Output

2. The general ledger account that would NOT appear in a post-closing trial balance would be　　　　　　2.____

    A. Cash   B. Accounts Payable
    C. Furniture and Fixtures   D. Sales Income

3. Ralph Hanley, age 45, supports his wife and three children.
Mr. Hanley is the only member of the family required to file an income tax return.
What is the MAXIMUM number of exemptions he can claim?　　　　　　3.____

    A. One   B. Five   C. Three   D. Four

4. The cost of a fixed asset minus the allowance for depreciation (accumulated depreciation) is the _____ value.　　　　　　4.____

    A. market   B. cost   C. liquidation   D. book

5. The form used by a bookkeeper in summarizing adjustments and information which will be used in preparing statements is called a　　　　　　5.____

    A. journal   B. balance sheet
    C. ledger   D. worksheet

6. When a large number of transactions of a particular kind are to be entered in bookkeeping records, it is USUALLY advisable to use　　　　　　6.____

    A. cash records   B. controlling accounts
    C. special journals   D. special ledgers

7. The petty cash book shows a petty cash balance of $9.80 on May 31. The petty cash box contains only $9.10.
What account will be debited to record the $.70 difference?　　　　　　7.____

    A. Cash   B. Petty Cash
    C. Cash Short and Over   D. Petty Cash Expense

8. The ONLY difference between the books of a partnership and those of a sole proprietorship appears in the _____ accounts.　　　　　　8.____

    A. proprietorship   B. liability
    C. asset   D. expense

9. The earnings of a corporation are FIRST recorded as a credit to an account called　　　　　　9.____

    A. Dividends Payable   B. Capital Stock Authorized
    C. Retained Earnings   D. Profit and Loss Summary

10. A firm purchased a new delivery truck for $2,900 and sold it four years later for $500. The Allowance for Depreciation of Delivery Equipment account was credited for $580 at the end of each of the four years.
When the machine was sold, there was a

    A. loss of $80
    B. loss of $1,820
    C. loss of $2,400
    D. gain of $80

10.____

11. FICA taxes are paid by

    A. employees *only*
    B. employers *only*
    C. both employees and employers
    D. neither employees nor employers

11.____

12. Which phase of the data processing cycle is the SAME as calculating net pay in a manual system?

    A. Input   B. Processing   C. Storing   D. Output

12.____

13. Which error will cause the trial balance to be out of balance?

    A. A sales invoice for $60 was entered in the Sales Journal for $600.
    B. A credit to office furniture in the journal was posted as a credit to office machines in the ledger.
    C. A debit to advertising expense in the journal was posted as a debit to miscellaneous expense in the ledger.
    D. A debit to office equipment in the journal was posted as a credit to office equipment in the ledger.

13.____

14. The collection of a bad debt previously written off will result in a(n)

    A. *decrease* in assets
    B. *decrease* in capital
    C. *increase* in assets
    D. *increase* in liabilities

14.____

15. Which account does NOT belong in the group?

    A. Notes Receivable
    B. Building
    C. Office Equipment
    D. Delivery Truck

15.____

16. The adjusting entry to record the estimated bad debts is debit _____ and credit _____.

    A. Allowance for Bad Debts; Bad Debts Expense
    B. Bad Debts Expense; Allowance for Bad Debts
    C. Allowance for Bad Debts; Accounts Receivable
    D. Bad Debts Expense; Accounts Receivable

16.____

17. At the end of the year, which account should be closed into the income and expense summary?

    A. Freight In
    B. Allowance for Doubtful Accounts
    C. Notes Receivable
    D. Petty Cash

17.____

18. Which form is prepared to aid in verifying that the customer's account balances in the customer's ledger agree with the balance in the Accounts Receivable account in the general ledger?   18.____

    A. Worksheet
    B. Schedule of Accounts Payable
    C. Schedule of Accounts Receivable
    D. Trial Balance

19. In the preparation of an income statement, failure to consider accrued wages will result in   19.____

    A. *overstating* operating expense and understating net profit
    B. *overstating* net profit *only*
    C. *understating* operating expense and overstating net profit
    D. *understating* operating expense *only*

20. The CORRECT formula for determining the rate of merchandise turnover is   20.____

    A. cost of goods sold divided by average inventory
    B. net sales divided by net purchases
    C. gross sales divided by ending inventory
    D. average inventory divided by cost of goods sold

21. A legal characteristic of a corporation is _____ liability.   21.____

    A. contingent   B. limited
    C. unlimited   D. deferred

22. A customer's check you had deposited is returned to you by the bank labeled *Dishonored*.   22.____
What entries would be made as a result of this action? Debit _____ and credit _____.

    A. cash; customer's account
    B. miscellaneous expense; cash
    C. customer's account; capital
    D. customer's account; cash

23. The TOTAL capital of a corporation may be found by adding   23.____

    A. assets and liabilities
    B. assets and capital stock
    C. liabilities and capital stock
    D. earned surplus and capital stock

24. The source of an entry made in the Petty Cash book is the   24.____

    A. general ledger   B. voucher
    C. register   D. general journal

25. Which account is debited to record interest earned but not yet due?   25.____

    A. Deferred Interest
    B. Interest Receivable
    C. Interest Income
    D. Income and Expense Summary

KEY (CORRECT ANSWERS)

1.	C		11.	C
2.	D		12.	B
3.	B		13.	D
4.	D		14.	C
5.	D		15.	A
6.	C		16.	B
7.	C		17.	A
8.	A		18.	C
9.	C		19.	C
10.	A		20.	A

21.	B
22.	D
23.	D
24.	B
25.	B

TEST 3

DIRECTIONS: Each question or incomplete statement is followed by several suggested answers or completions. Select the one that BEST answers the question or completes the statement. *PRINT THE LETTER OF THE CORRECT ANSWER IN THE SPACE AT THE RIGHT.*

1. Which reason should NOT generally be used by an employer when making a hiring decision?
An applicant('s)

   A. resume reveals a lack of job-related skills
   B. attendance record on a previous job is poor
   C. has improperly prepared the job application
   D. is married

   1.____

2. Graves, Owens, and Smith formed a partnership and invested $15,000 each. If the firm made a profit of $18,000 last year and profits and losses were shared equally, what was Owens' share of the net profit?

   A. $1,000 B. $5,000 C. $6,000 D. $9,000

   2.____

3. The bank statement balance of the Bedford Co. on May 31 was $3,263.28. The checkbook balance was $3,119.06. A reconciliation showed that the outstanding checks totaled $147.22 and that there was a bank service charge of $3.00. The CORRECT checkbook balance should be

   A. $3,260.28 B. $3,122.06 C. $3,116.06 D. $3,266.28

   3.____

4. Which account is shown in a post-closing trial balance?

   A. Prepaid Insurance B. Fees Income
   C. Purchases D. Freight In

   4.____

5. A check endorsed *For deposit only (signed) Samuel Jones* is an example of a _____ endorsement.

   A. full B. blank C. complete D. restrictive

   5.____

6. The selling price of a share of stock as published in a daily newspaper is called the _____ value.

   A. book B. face C. par D. market

   6.____

7. Which is obtained by dividing the cost of goods sold by the average inventory?

   A. Current ratio
   B. Merchandise inventory turnover
   C. Average rate of mark-up
   D. Acid-test ratio

   7.____

8. A Suzuki truck costing $39,000 is expected to have a useful life of six years and a salvage value of $3,000.
If $6,000 is debited to the depreciation expense account each year for six years, what method of depreciation is used?

   A. Units of production B. Straight line
   C. Declining balance D. Sum of the years digits

   8.____

9. Which form is prepared to aid in verifying that the customer's account balances in the
customer's ledger agree with the balance in the Accounts Receivable account in the
General Ledger?

    A. Worksheet
    B. Schedule of Accounts Payable
    C. Schedule of Accounts Receivable
    D. Trial Balance

9.____

10. In the preparation of a balance sheet, failure to consider commissions owed to salesper-
sons will result in _____ liabilities and _____ capital.

    A. understating; overstating
    B. understating; understating
    C. overstating; overstating
    D. overstating; understating

10.____

11. A financial statement generated by a computer is an example of a(n)

    A. audit trail   B. output
    C. input   D. program

11.____

12. Merchandise was sold for $150 cash plus a 3% sales tax.
The CORRECT credit(s) should be

    A. Sales Income $150, Sales Taxes Payable $4.50
    B. Sales Income $154.50
    C. Merchandise $150, Sales Taxes Payable $4.50
    D. Sales Income $150

12.____

13. The bookkeeper should prepare a bank reconciliation MAINLY to determine

    A. which checks are outstanding
    B. whether the checkbook balance and the bank statement balance are in agreement
    C. the total amount of checks written during the month
    D. the total amount of cash deposited during the month

13.____

14. Which is the CORRECT procedure for calculating the rate of merchandise turnover?

    A. Gross Sales divided by Net Sales
    B. Cost of Goods Sold divided by Average Inventory
    C. Net Purchases divided by Average Inventory
    D. Gross Purchases divided by Net Purchases

14.____

15. Which previous job should be listed FIRST on a job application form?
The

    A. least recent job   B. most recent job
    C. job you liked best   D. job which paid the most

15.____

16. Failure to record cash sales will result in

    A. *overstatement* of profit
    B. *understatement* of profit
    C. *understatement* of liabilities
    D. *overstatement* of capital

16.____

17. When a fixed asset is repaired, the cost of the repairs should be _____ account.　　17._____

    A. *debited* to the asset
    B. *debited* to the expense
    C. *credited* to the proprietor's capital
    D. *credited* to the asset

18. The form used by a bookkeeper to summarize information which will be used in preparing financial statements is called a　　18._____

    A. journal　　　　　　　　　　B. balance sheet
    C. ledger　　　　　　　　　　D. worksheet

19. Which type of ledger account is a summary of a number of accounts in another ledger?　　19._____
_____ account.

    A. Controlling　　　　　　　　B. Subsidiary
    C. Asset　　　　　　　　　　D. Proprietorship

20. What is the summary entry on the Purchases Journal?　　20._____
Debit _____ and credit _____.

    A. Accounts Payable; Merchandise Purchases
    B. Accounts Receivable; Merchandise Purchases
    C. Merchandise Purchases; Accounts Receivable
    D. Merchandise Purchases; Accounts Payable

21. The source document for entries made in the Sales Journal is a(n)　　21._____

    A. credit memo　　　　　　　　B. statement of accounts
    C. invoice　　　　　　　　　　D. bill of lading

22. A Trial Balance which is in balance would NOT reveal the　　22._____

    A. omission of the credit part of an entry
    B. posting of the same debit twice
    C. omission of an entire transaction
    D. omission of an account with a balance

23. A financial statement prepared by a computerized accounting system is an example of　　23._____

    A. input　　　　　　　　　　B. output
    C. flowcharting　　　　　　　D. programming

24. The form which the payroll clerk gives to each employee to show gross earnings and taxes withheld for the year is a　　24._____

    A. W-2　　　　B. W-3　　　　C. W-4　　　　D. 1040

25. Who would be the LEAST appropriate reference on an application for a job?　　25._____
A

    A. relative
    B. guidance counselor
    C. former employer
    D. prominent member of the community

KEY (CORRECT ANSWERS)

1.	D		11.	B
2.	C		12.	A
3.	C		13.	B
4.	A		14.	B
5.	D		15.	B
6.	D		16.	B
7.	B		17.	B
8.	B		18.	D
9.	C		19.	A
10.	A		20.	D

21.	C
22.	C
23.	B
24.	A
25.	A

———

EXAMINATION SECTION

TEST 1

1. A line of a Federal Income Tax Rate Schedule reads: 1.___
    over   but not over   your tax is:
    $6,000 $8,000 $1,130 plus 25% of excess over $6,000.
    The income tax due on taxable income of $7,200 is
       A. $1,130   B. $1,430   C. $1,630   D. $1,800

2. We discounted at our bank a customer's promissory note for   2.___
    $3,000. The proceeds were $2,985.
    The CORRECT credit part of the entry to record this trans-
    action is
       A. Notes Payable, $3,000
       B. Notes Receivable Discounted, $3,000
       C. Notes Payable, $2,985
       D. Notes Receivable Discounted, $2,985

3. A payment for gasoline and oil was incorrectly debited to   3.___
    the Delivery Equipment account instead of to the Delivery
    Expense account.
    This error, if not corrected, would result in
       A. an overstatement of the net profit
       B. an understatement of the net profit
       C. no change in the net profit
       D. no change in the total assets

4. A federal depository receipt is issued when a firm   4.___
       A. reports to an employee the amount of federal taxes
          withheld from his wages during the year
       B. purchases United States government bonds
       C. deposits its surplus cash in a bank
       D. deposits in a bank FICA taxes and federal withholding
          taxes

5. As evidence of part ownership in a corporation, a person   5.___
    receives a
       A. certificate of incorporation
       B. stock certificate
       C. bond
       D. charter

6. One advantage resulting from the use of controlling   6.___
    accounts in the general ledger is that fewer
       A. bookkeepers are needed to do the work
       B. pages are needed in each journal
       C. accounts are needed in the subsidiary ledgers
       D. postings are required in the general ledger

7. The proprietor took home an office desk from the business   7.___
   for his personal use.
   The effect on the fundamental bookkeeping equation is to
      A. *increase* assets, decrease owner's worth
      B. *increase* assets, increase liabilities
      C. *increase* assets, increase owner's worth
      D. *decrease* owner's worth, decrease assets

8. Which can be determined from information found on the   8.___
   Balance Sheet?
      A. Current ratio
      B. Ratio of net profit to sales
      C. Total operating expenses
      D. Total income

9. In recording the amount of State sales tax collected on   9.___
   cash sales, the amount to be credited is
      A. Sales   B. Sales Taxes Payable
      C. Sales Taxes Receivable   D. Sales Taxes Expense

10. The rate of return on capital investment is found by   10.___
    dividing the amount of investment into
       A. total sales   B. proprietor's drawings
       C. net income   D. total current assets

Questions 11-15.

DIRECTIONS: Questions 11 through 15 are to be answered on the basis
of the following account.

DATE		EXPLANATION	POST. REF.	- DEBIT	CREDIT	BALANCE
May	3		J 21	630 00		630 00
	7		M 11		25 00	605 00
	10		CR 34		605 00	
June	13		J 32	230 00		230 00
	15		M 27	15 00		245 00

Name: Grey-Jackson, Inc.   Terms: 2/10, N/30
Address: 75 E. 43, New York, N.Y. 10017

11. This account will be found in   11.___
       A. Accounts Receivable Subsidiary
       B. Accounts Payable Subsidiary
       C. General
       D. Sales

12. From which business paper did the entry on May 3 originate?   12.___
    A
      .A. purchases invoice   B. shipping memo
       C. sales invoice   D. statement of account

13. The MOST probable reason for the entry on May 7 is that   13.____
    A. a partial payment was made
    B. merchandise was returned
    C. a cash discount on the transaction of May 3 was
       allowed
    D. shipping charges were prepaid

14. In order to obtain more information regarding the entry   14.____
    of May 7, the bookkeeper should refer to
    A. invoice number 11
    B. page 11 of the Grey-Jackson, Inc. file
    C. the 11th entry in the General Journal
    D. page 11 of the General Journal

15. If the debit on June 15 represents a freight charge, how   15.____
    much should be paid on June 22?
    A. $245.00   B. $240.40   C. $240.10   D. $230.00

16. Which error will cause the Trial Balance to be out of   16.____
    balance?
    The
    A. bookkeeper charged an item to Miscellaneous Expense
       instead of to Advertising Expense
    B. bookkeeper failed to post an entire entry from the
       General Journal
    C. bookkeeper incorrectly entered the amount of a
       purchase into the Purchases Journal
    D. Petty Cash account was omitted from the Trial Balance

17. On October 14, the bookkeeper received in the mail a   17.____
    customer's check for $500. The identical amount, $500,
    is also due to a creditor on October 14.
    Which is the recommended bookkeeping procedure?
    A. Endorse the check to the creditor, and mail it to him.
    B. Request your firm's bank to certify the customer's
       check, and mail it to your creditor.
    C. Deposit the customer's check, and mail a separate
       check to the creditor.
    D. Return the customer's check to him, and request him
       to mail it to the creditor.

18. A sale is made on June 16, terms 2/10, EOM.   18.____
    In order for the discount to be allowed, payment must be
    made no later than
    A. June 26   B. June 30   C. July 2   D. July 10

19. When a petty cash fund is established, the effect on the   19.____
    fundamental accounting equation is that total assets
    A. and total liabilities remain unchanged
    B. decrease; total liabilities increase
    C. decrease; proprietorship decreases
    D. increase; proprietorship increases

20. One of the reasons for preparing a Schedule of Accounts   20.___
    Receivable is to
    A. make up statements of customers accounts
    B. determine if the subsidiary ledger agrees with the
       controlling account
    C. determine the worth of the business
    D. determine the total sales for the fiscal period

21. The current price of a share of stock traded on the   21.___
    stock exchange is called the _____ value.
    A. market   B. par   C. book   D. face

22. In a certain industry, firm A had a current ratio of 4:1;   22.___
    while firm B had a current ratio of 1:1.
    A logical conclusion would be that firm A
    A. had a higher merchandise turnover than firm B
    B. had more cash than firm B
    C. had more assets than firm B
    D. was better able to pay its current debts than firm B

23. When a bank certifies a $100 check for the person who   23.___
    wrote the check, it
    A. pays $100 to the person who wrote the check
    B. tells the depositor that he should remember this
       check so as to avoid overdrawing his account
    C. immediately deducts the $100 from the balance of the
       account
    D. asks the depositor for $100 to cover the check

24. A 90-day, 6% interest-bearing note for $340 was paid on   24.___
    the due date.
    The amount of the check was
    A. $345.10   B. $343.40   C. $340.00   D. $334.90

25. The declaration by a corporation of dividend to be paid   25.___
    at a future date results in a decrease in
    A. assets and a decrease in net worth
    B. assets and an increase in liabilities
    C. liabilities and a decrease in net worth
    D. net worth and an increase in liabilities

KEY (CORRECT ANSWERS)

1. B	6. D	11. A	16. D	21. A
2. B	7. D	12. D	17. B	22. D
3. A	8. A	13. B	18. D	23. C
4. D	9. B	14. D	19. A	24. A
5. B	10. C	15. B	20. B	25. D

TEST 2

DIRECTIONS: Each question or incomplete statement is followed by
several suggested answers or completions. Select the
one that BEST answers the question or completes the
statement. *PRINT THE LETTER OF THE CORRECT ANSWER IN
THE SPACE AT THE RIGHT.*

1. Which can be determined from information found on the   1.___
    Balance Sheet?
    A. Current ratio
    B. Rate of net profit based on sales
    C. Merchandise turnover
    D. Total operating expenses

2. Which statement BEST describes the function of a source   2.___
    document in an automatic data processing system?
    A. Input is recorded on it.
    B. Output is recorded on it.
    C. Raw data is obtained from it.
    D. It manipulates the central processing unit.

3. Postings to the debit side of Accounts Payable in the   3.___
    General Ledger USUALLY come from the _____ Journal.
    A. Cash Payments   B. Sales
    C. Purchases   D. Cash Receipts

4. The PRIMARY purpose of a trial balance is to   4.___
    A. check the accuracy of control accounts
    B. locate errors in posting
    C. assure the accuracy of financial reports
    D. determine if the general ledger is in balance

5. An outstanding check is a check that has   5.___
    A. been voided   B. been deposited
    C. not been written   D. not been paid

6. If the total of the credit column on the Income Statement   6.___
    of the worksheet is larger than the total of the debit
    column, the difference is called net
    A. income   B. loss   C. worth   D. value

7. Which is NOT an input device in an electronic data   7.___
    processing system?
    A(n)
    A. optical scanner   B. magnetic tape unit
    C. printer   D. console keyboard

8. After all closing entries are recorded and posted, the   8.___
    _____ account would still have a balance.
    A. Income and Expense Summary
    B. Purchases
    C. Owner's Drawing
    D. Owner's Capital

9. Failure to replenish Petty Cash at the end of the fiscal   9.___
   period will result in
   A. *understatement* of Net Income
   B. *overstatement* of Net Income
   C. *understatement* of Petty Cash
   D. *overstatement* of Expenses

10. Which item should NOT appear on a job application form?   10.___
    A. Current address   B. Social security number
    C. Religion   D. Education

11. If a person holds a civil service job, he or she is   11.___
    employed by
    A. the government
    B. a private accounting firm
    C. a large engineering firm
    D. a nonprofit charitable organization

12. Which is NOT given by an employer to an employee as a   12.___
    fringe benefit?
    A. Paid vacation days
    B. Paid sick leave
    C. Group life insurance coverage
    D. Payment of federal income taxes

13. A source of current job openings is(are)   13.___
    A. DICTIONARY OF OCCUPATIONAL TITLES
    B. CAREER INFORMATION HANDBOOK
    C. classified advertisements in a newspaper
    D. OCCUPATIONAL OUTLOOK HANDBOOK

14. Which reason should NOT generally be used by an employer   14.___
    when making a hiring decision?
    An applicant('s)
    A. resume reveals a lack of job-related skills
    B. attendance record on a previous job is poor
    C. has improperly prepared the job application
    D. is married

15. When listing previous jobs on an employment application,   15.___
    the prospective employer should list his/her _____ job first.
    A. least recent   B. most recent
    C. favorite   D. highest salaried

16. The LEAST appropriate reference on an application for a   16.___
    job would be a
    A. relative
    B. guidance counselor
    C. former employer
    D. prominent member of the community

17. Receipt of a $300 check from a customer in payment of   17.___
    his $300 account results in
       A. an increase in total value of assets
       B. a decrease in total value of assets
       C. no change in total value of assets
       D. an increase in net worth

18. The monthly report sent to each customer to remind him of   18.___
    the amount he owes is called a(n)
       A. invoice   B. statement of account
       C. bank statement   D. credit memorandum

19. Entries in the Cash Payments Journal are USUALLY made   19.___
    from
       A. Sales Invoices   B. Petty Cash Vouchers
       C. Checkbook stubs   D. Purchase orders

20. The Petty Cash book shows a petty cash balance of $10 on   20.___
    June 30. An actual count of the petty cash on hand on
    June 30 shows $9.00 in the petty cash box.
    The account to be debited to record the difference between
    the book balance and the petty cash on hand would be
       A. Petty Cash   B. Cash
       C. Cash Short and Over   D. Petty Cash Expense

KEY (CORRECT ANSWERS)

1. A		11. A	
2. C		12. D	
3. A		13. C	
4. D		14. D	
5. D		15. B	
6. A		16. A	
7. C		17. C	
8. D		18. B	
9. B		19. C	
10. C		20. C	

TEST 3

DIRECTIONS: Each question or incomplete statement is followed by several suggested answers or completions. Select the one that BEST answers the question or completes the statement. *PRINT THE LETTER OF THE CORRECT ANSWER IN THE SPACE AT THE RIGHT.*

1. Information prepared in machine-readable form for processing by automatic data processing equipment is commonly referred to as
   A. output
   B. business data
   C. input
   D. financial data

   1.____

2. Mr. H. Brown, the owner of a small business, withdrew money for his own use. The bookkeeper debited the H. Brown Capital account and credited the Cash account. To correct this error, the bookkeeper should debit the ____ account and credit the ____ account.
   A. H. Brown Personal; H. Brown Capital
   B. H. Brown Personal; Cash
   C. Cash; H. Brown Personal
   D. H. Brown Capital; H. Brown Personal

   2.____

3. The Dale Corporation earned a net profit of $50,000 for the year. Before closing the books, the Capital Stock account showed a balance of $300,000, and the Retained Earnings account had a balance of $40,000.
   The net worth of the firm on December 31 was
   A. $340,000   B. $350,000   C. $390,000   D. $310,000

   3.____

4. An example of a machine commonly used to record data on cards in machine-readable form for use in an automatic data processing system is the
   A. typewriter
   B. electric billing machine
   C. office copying machine
   D. key punch

   4.____

5. The receipt of a check in settlement of an interest-bearing note will result in an increase in assets(,)
   A. and a decrease in assets
   B. a decrease in assets, and an increase in capital
   C. a decrease in assets, and a decrease in capital
   D. a decrease in liabilities, and an increase in capital

   5.____

6. A sale on credit to George Rogers for $200 was incorrectly posted to his account as $20.
   This error would mean that the
   A. Schedule of Accounts Receivable would be understated
   B. Accounts Receivable controlling account would be over-stated
   C. Schedule of Accounts Receivable would be overstated
   D. trial balance would not balance

   6.____

7. A cash sale of $250 worth of merchandise subject to a 6% sales tax should be recorded as a debit to the Cash account for   7.___
   A. $250 and a credit to the Sales Income account for $250
   B. $265 and a credit to the Sales Income account for $265
   C. $250, a debit to the Sales Tax Expense account for $15, and a credit to the Sales Income account for $265
   D. a credit to the Sales Income account for $250, and a credit to the Sales Taxes Payable account for $15

8. To determine which checks are outstanding at the end of each month, the bookkeeper should   8.___
   A. ask the bank to send a list of these outstanding checks
   B. find the necessary information in the bank statement
   C. compare the cancelled checks with the bank statement
   D. compare the cancelled checks with the checkbook stubs

9. An error was made in writing the amount of a check. The BEST business procedure to be followed is to   9.___
   A. cross off the incorrect amount on the check and neatly write the correct amount above the incorrect figure
   B. erase the incorrect amount on the check and neatly fill in the correct amount
   C. write *void* across the check and the stub and write a new check
   D. tear up the check and write a new check

10. When a posting machine is used, Accounts Receivable and Accounts Payable are USUALLY kept in a   10.___
   A. bound ledger with money columns for debit and credit
   B. looseleaf ledger with money columns for debit and credit
   C. card ledger with money columns for debit, credit, and balance
   D. bound ledger with money columns for debit, credit, and balance

11. The federal individual income tax return MUST be filed by   11.___
   A. December 31   B. March 15
   C. April 15   D. June 30

12. When cash is received as a result of sales, the PROPER business procedure is to   12.___
   A. put the cash in the petty cash box
   B. deposit the cash in a checking account at the end of the day
   C. deposit the cash in a savings account at the end of the day
   D. use the cash to pay current bills

13. When figuring extensions on invoices, the machine that   13.___
    would be MOST helpful would be a _____ machine.
    · A. full keyboard adding   B. mimeograph
      C. key punch   D. calculating

14. The bookkeeper failed to record depreciation for the year. 14.___
    As a result, the
        A. assets will be understated
        B. profit will be understated
        C. profit will be overstated
        D. liabilities will be overstated

15. The TOTAL of the Schedule of Accounts Receivable should   15.___
    agree with the
        A. total of the Accounts Receivable column in the cash
           receipts journal
        B. total of the Accounts Receivable column in the general
           journal
        C. balance of the Accounts Receivable controlling account
        D. balance in the Sales account

16. Which error would cause the trial balance to be out of   16.___
    balance?
        A. Incorrectly totaling the Sales Journal
        B. Failing to post to a customer's account from the Sales
           Journal
        C. Incorrectly debiting the Office Expense account
           instead of the Furniture and Fixtures account
        D. Incorrectly adding the debits in the Notes Payable
           account

17. The business paper which is used as a source for an entry   17.___
    in the Petty Cash book is a
        A. voucher   B. purchase order
        C. check stub   D. credit memorandum

18. On December 31, the Capital Stock account of the Rogers   18.___
    Corporation showed a balance of $75,000, and the Retained
    Earnings account showed a balance of $15,000.
    If 1,000 shares of stock were in the hands of stockholders,
    the book value of each share of stock was
        A. $90   B. $75   C. $60   D. 15

19. A 60-day promissory note dated July 7 will be due on   19.___
        A. August 6   B. September 5
        C. September 6   D. September 7

20. A bank reconciliation showed a deposit in transit, a bank   20.___
    charge, outstanding checks, and a certified outstanding
    check.
    On the basis of this information, the bookkeeper should
    make an entry to record the
        A. deposit in transit   B. bank charge
        C. outstanding checks   D. certified outstanding check

21. Merchandise was sold on February 8 for $175 less a trade 21.____
    discount of 20%, terms 2/10, n/30.
    The amount of the check received on March 9 should be
       A. $137.20   B. $140.00   C. $171.50   D. $175.00

22. The monthly report sent by a bank to a depositor showing 22.____
    his balance in the bank, deposits made during the month,
    and checks paid during the month is called a
       A. bank reconciliation   B. monthly report
       C. bank statement   D. balance sheet

23. A $200 check received from John Howard, a customer, in 23.____
    payment of his $200 promissory note was entered incorrectly
    by debiting the Cash account and crediting the John Howard
    account.
    The CORRECTING entry should debit the _____ account and
    credit the _____ account.
       A. Cash; Notes Receivable
       B. Notes Receivable; John Howard
       C. John Howard; Notes Receivable
       D. Cash; John Howard

24. Bond holders of a corporation are _____ of the corporation. 24.____
       A. owners   B. creditors   C. customers   D. directors

25. Which error will cause the trial balance to be out of 25.____
    balance?
       A. Posting to the wrong side of a customer's account
          in the Accounts Receivable Ledger
       B. Failure to record a sale in the Sales Journal
       C. Totaling the Purchase Journal incorrectly
       D. Posting a $1,450 debit to the Accounts Payable
          controlling account as $1,540

KEY (CORRECT ANSWERS)

1. C		11. C	
2. A		12. B	
3. C		13. D	
4. D		14. C	
5. B		15. C	
6. A		16. D	
7. D		17. A	
8. D		18. A	
9. C		19. B	
10. C		20. B	

21. B
22. C
23. C
24. B
25. D

BOOKKEEPING PROBLEMS
EXAMINATION SECTION
TEST 1

Questions 1-25.
DIRECTIONS:

Below you will find the *CASH RECEIPTS JOURNAL* of John Walker, a merchant.

Under the heading of each money column of the Journals, there is a letter of the alphabet.

Following the Journals there is a series of transactions.

You are to determine the entry for each transaction and then show in the space on the right *the columns to be used.*

For example: If a certain transaction entered in the *CASH RECEIPTS JOURNAL* results in an entry of $100 in the General Ledger Column and $100 in the Net Cash Column, in the appropriate space on the right, you should write: A, E. If the record of the transaction requires the use of more than two columns, your answer should contain more than two letters.

DO NOT PUT THE AMOUNTS IN YOUR ANSWER SPACE. The *letters* of the columns in the Cash Journals to be used are sufficient.

If a transaction requires no entry in the Cash Journals, write "None" in the appropriate space on the right, even though a record would be made in some other journal.

CASH RECEIPTS JOURNAL

Date	Account Credited	Explana-tion	F	General Ledger	Accts. Rec.	Cash Sales	Disc. on Sales	Net Cash
				A	B	C	D	E

CASH PAYMENTS JOURNAL

Date	Acct. Debited	Explana-tion	F	General Ledger	Accts. Pay.	Soc. Sec. Taxes Pay.	With. Taxes Pay.	Disc. on Purch.	Net Cash
				F	G	H	I	J	K

1. Cash Sales amounted to $280.   1. ....
2. Paid employees salaries for the week. The check amounted   2. ....
   to $346 after deducting $4.00 for Social Security Taxes and
   $30 for Income Taxes withheld.
3. A check received in the mail from R. Walters was in payment   3. ....
   of a bill of $150, terms 2/10, n/30. The customer had taken
   the discount.
4. The proprietor, Mr. Walker, took merchandise valued at $30   4. ....
   from the stock room for his personal use.
5. Prepaid $15 freight on shipment of goods to H. Lane, a   5. ....
   customer, and charged his account.
6. Sent a check for $250 to P. Packer to apply on account.   6. ....
7. Drew a check for $75 to start a Petty Cash fund.   7. ....

1

8. H. Wall sent us a check for $700 in payment of his 60-day   8. ....
   note for $700. The note was interest bearing (6%) but he
   failed to pay us the interest. We deposited the $700 check
   and wrote to him requesting an additional check.

9. Paid rent for month $180.   9. ....

10. Received a check for $70 from K. London to apply on ac-   10. ....
   count.

11. H. Wall sent us a check for the interest due on note (see   11. ....
   item 8).

12. Paid our 30-day note for $460 due today which we had given 12. ....
   to G. Thompson.

13. Accepted a trade acceptance drawn by R. Sparks on us for   13. ....
   invoice of $722.

14. Borrowed at our bank on our $1500 note. Net proceeds,   14. ....
   $1485. (The bookkeeper used only one journal to make a
   complete and correct entry. You are to do likewise.)

15. Received a check for $60 from W. Saks, a creditor, refund- 15. ....
   ing our overpayment to him on our account.

16. A check from H. Low which was deposited by us last month 16. ....
   was returned to us marked "insufficient funds." The check
   amounted to $55 and had been sent to us to settle his ac-
   count.

17. Drew a sight draft on R. Coe for overdue account of $120. 17. ....
   Left draft at bank for collection.

18. Paid $26 freight on goods purchased from W. Lincoln of   18. ....
   Chicago, terms f.o.b. Chicago.

19. Mailed a credit memorandum to E. Stern for return of de- 19. ....
   fective merchandise sold him on account for $65.

20. The proprietor, John Walker, drew $90 cash for personal 20. ....
   use.

21. Received a money order for $110 from B. Kiner for invoice 21. ....
   of merchandise charged to him.

22. Mr. Walker, proprietor, drew $1200 from his personal sav- 22. ....
   ings account and invested the entire sum in his business.

23. Issued check to Clark & Co. in payment of invoice amount- 23. ....
   ing to $500. Discount of 3% was taken.

24. Received a 30-day non-interest bearing note for $610 from 24. ....
   A. Allen for merchandise sold him today.

25. Sent a check for $51 to Collector of Internal Revenue for 25. ....
   Social Security Taxes collected for the past three months.

Questions 26-35.

DIRECTIONS:

   Below you will find the *GENERAL JOURNAL* used by D. Prince, wholesaler.

   Under the heading of each money column you will find a letter of the
alphabet.

   Following the *GENERAL JOURNAL* there is a series of transactions.

   You are to determine the correct entry for each transaction and then
show in the appropriate space on the right, the columns to be used.

   For example, if a certain transaction results in an entry of $100 in
the Notes Receivable Column (on the left side) and an entry of $100 in
the General Ledger Column (on the right side), in the appropriate space
on the right, you should write A, D.

   If the record of the transaction requires the use of more than two
columns, your answer should contain more than two letters.

   DO NOT PUT THE AMOUNTS ON YOUR ANSWER SPACE. The *letters* of the
columns to be used are sufficient.

If a transaction requires no entry in the *GENERAL JOURNAL*, write "None" in the appropriate space on the right, even though a record would be made in some other journal.

GENERAL JOURNAL

Notes Rec.	Accts. Pay.	General Ledger	L. F.		General Ledger	Accts. Rec.	Notes Payable
A	B	C			D	E	F

26. Issued a credit memorandum for $68 to J. Winston for goods returned to us.   26. ....
27. P. Jones sent us his 60-day note for $750 in full settlement of his account   27. ....
28. Sent a 60-day note to J. O'Connor for invoice of $375 less 2%.   28. ....
29. H. Owens sent us a credit memorandum for overcharge of $75 on invoice.   29. ....
30. Mailed a 30-day draft to W. Kinder, a customer, for his acceptance amounting to $375 for invoice of goods sold him yesterday.   30. ....
31. A. Hocker, a customer, went out of business owing us $170. The claim is considered worthless.   31. ....
32. The proprietor requested the bookkeeper to provide a reserve of $500 for expected losses on customers' accounts.   32. ....
33. P. Winston sent us a $350 bank draft in full settlement of his account.   33. ....
34. Accepted a 30-day trade acceptance drawn by A. Hall for bill of goods amounting to $316 purchased by us last week.   34. ....
35. Mr. D. Prince, the proprietor, takes his brother, L. Prince, into the business as an equal partner. Mr. L. Prince invests merchandise worth $3500 in the business and becomes a partner.

Questions 36-50.

DIRECTIONS:

Below you will find a list of accounts from the ledger of R. Lincoln. There is a letter of the alphabet before each account.

A. Accounts Payable
B. Accounts Receivable
C. Cash
D. Delivery Expense
E. Discount on Purchases
F. Freight Inward
G. Interest Cost
H. Purchases
I. Notes Receivable
J. Notes Receivable Discounted
K. Notes Payable
L. Office Supplies
M. R. Lincoln, Personal
N. Petty Cash
O. Purchase Returns
P. Sales Discount
R. Sales Returns
S. Sales Income

Using the letter in front of each account title (using no accounts not listed), make journal entries for the transactions given below.

Do not write the names of the accounts in your answer space. Simply indicate in the proper space on the right the letters of the accounts to be debited or credited.

Always give the letter or letters of accounts to be debited *first*, *then* give the letter or letters of accounts to be credited.

For example, if Office Supplies and Delivery Expenses are to be debited and Notes Payable and Cash are to be credited in a certain transaction, then write as your answer L, D; K, C.

36. Paid the Fox Transportation Co. $15 by check for express charges on goods delivered to us.   36. ....
37. Accepted a 30-day trade acceptance for $850 drawn on us by Allen & Co.   37. ....
38. Returned damaged goods to H. Parker and he sent us a credit memorandum for $47.   38. ....
39. John Smith's 30-day note for $800, which was discounted by us at our bank last month, was paid by him today.   39. ....
40. Paid our 60-day note due today in favor of S. Paul for $600 with interest. The check amounted to $606.   40. ....
41. The total of the Notes Payable column in the General Journal amounted to $450 at the end of last month. It was posted in error to the Notes Receivable Discounted account. Make the correction entry.   41. ....
42. Issued a check to J. News in settlement of invoice $500 less 2%.   42. ....
43. Paid Stern Stationers $5.00 by check for four reams of paper for office use.   43. ....
44. Sent a check for $48 to Gregory's Garage for storage, gasoline, oil and service on auto trucks.   44. ....
45. Drew a check for $100 to establish a Petty Cash fund.   45. ....
46. A. Black, a customer, settled his account of $400 by sending us a check for $100 and a 30-day note for the balance.   46. ....
47. J. Walters failed to deduct a discount of $10 when he paid us last month. He called the matter to our attention and we sent him a check for $10.   47. ....
48. Donated to the Salvation Army merchandise out of stock costing the proprietor $75.   48. ....
49. At the end of the year the Sales Returns account had a balance of $225. Make the entry to close this account.   49. ....
50. At the end of the year the Freight Inward account had a balance of $450. Make the entry to close this account.   50. ...

Questions 51-60.
DIRECTIONS:
   In Questions 51 to 60, place the *CORRECT* answer in the space at the right.

51. On December 31, a bookkeeper prepared a Profit and Loss   51. ....
Statement in which the following are some of the items listed:

Sales	$50,000
Purchases	45,000
Inventory (Jan. 1)	7,500
Sales Returns	400
Gross Profit	15,000
Selling Expense	3,200

Find the Inventory of Merchandise on December 31.
52. A. Landers invested $5,000 in cash in a new business. At   52. ....
the end of the year he finds he has $2,500 in cash, $1,000 in furniture, $1,800 in merchandise on which he owes $750. During the year, Mr. Landers drew $2,400 for his own use. What was his profit or loss for the year? (Write P or L before the figure.)
53. Wm. Abbott purchased a machine for $2,800. The estimated   53. ....
life of the machine was five years. At the end of five years the machine could be sold for scrap for $400. Find the depreciation charge at the end of the first six months of use.

54. On January 1, A. Menton's Capital was $2,400. His partner, 54. .....
    P. King, had a Capital of $6,000. Their agreement provided
    for dividing profits in proportion to Capital. During the
    year the Net Profit was $12,480.
    What was A. Menton's share of the Net Profit?

55. On December 31, J. Klein's ledger, after all closing en-   55. .....
    tries, contained the following balances:

Cash	$ 5,000
Merchandise Inventory	1,500
Accounts Receivable	8,000
Notes Receivable	2,000
Deferred Expense	300
Furniture and Fixtures	1,200
Accounts Payable	4,000
Reserve for Bad Debts	600
Notes Receivable Discounted	800
Reserve for Depreciation of Furniture and Fixtures	900

What was J. Klein's Capital on December 31?

56. An employer paid $160 in Social Security taxes at the rate 56. .....
    of 1% on taxable wages. He expects to employ more persons
    next year and pay out 50% more in taxable wages than he did.
    What will be his Social Security costs at the new rate of
    1 1/2% next year?

57. On June 17 you discounted a customer's 60-day note at your 57. .....
    bank. The face of the note was $840 and it was dated
    June 5, discount rate 6%.
    What was the amount of the net proceeds?

58. On June 18 you sold I. Cohen, of Chicago, merchandise.   58. .....
    The invoice totaled $684, which included $38 freight which
    you had prepaid. Terms were 2, 10, n/30, f.o.b. New York.
    If Mr. Cohen pays you on June 27, what should be the *correct*
    amount of the check?

59. A bankrupt firm agrees to pay its creditors 30 cents on   59. .....
    the dollar. It pays Klein & Co. $12,600.
    What was Klein & Co.'s loss?

60. A salesman earned $15,600 in one year. His commissions   60. .....
    were at the rate of 7 1/2% of Sales.
    What were his sales for the year?

Questions 61-80.
DIRECTIONS:
    Questions 61 to 80 are based on the following:
    The bookkeeper of Walters Co. began to make a trial balance of his
General Ledger on December 31. Before he had completed his trial
balance, you were permitted to examine his work.
    If a balance is in the correct column, write "C" in the appropriate
space on the right. If a balance is in the wrong column, write "W" in
the appropriate space on the right.
    Caution: Since the trial balance is not complete, do not attempt
              to strike a balance of the figures given in the question.

WALTER CO.
Trial Balance, December 31

61. Merchandise, Inventory, Jan. 1	16,000		61. ....
62. Freight Inward		150	62. ....
63. Petty Cash		75	63. ....

64.	Interest Income		70	64. ....
65.	Notes Receivable		4,000	65. ....
66.	Sales	17,000		66. ....
67.	Sales Discount	170		67. ....
68.	Purchase Returns		250	68. ....
69.	Auto Trucks		9,000	69. ....
70.	Reserve for Depreciation of Furniture		770	70. ....
71.	Bad Debts	160		71. ....
72.	Sales Taxes Collected		225	72. ....
73.	Sales Returns	485		73. ....
74.	Reserve for Bad Debts	500		74. ....
75.	Deposits with Landlord	150		75. ....
76.	Accrued Interest on Notes Receivable	50		76. ....
77.	Income from Commissions	900		77. ....
78.	Purchase Discounts	110		78. ....
79.	Depreciation of Furniture	225		79. ....
80.	Notes and Acceptances from Customers	780		80. ....

TEST 2

Questions 1-25.

DIRECTIONS:

Below you will find:
1. General ledger balances on January 31, appearing in books of A. New.
2. All entries on books of A. New for month of February.
3. You are to supply balances of ledger accounts on February 29, in the appropriate spaces on the right, as indicated at the end of these questions.

The correct balances in A. New's general ledger on January 31 were as follows: Cash $7642; Notes Receivable $2600; Accounts Receivable $3100; Furniture and Fixtures $750; Delivery Equipment $1200; Purchases $2850; Telephone and Telegrams $110; Office Supplies $380; Salaries $300; Sales Discount $80; Purchase Discount $56; Insurance $160; Sales $3150; Freight Inward $70; Accounts Payable $2400; Freight Outward (debit) $40; Notes Payable $1100; A. New Capital $12200; A. New Personal (credit) $310; Sales Taxes Payable $35; Withholding Taxes Payable $28; and Social Security Taxes Payable $3.

CASH RECEIPTS

Date	Name	Net Cash	Sales Disc.	Accts. Rec.	Miscellaneous Account	Amount
2/2	S. Wilson	471.00	9.00	480.00		
2/5	First Nat'l Bank	500.00			Notes Pay.	500.00
2/16	M. Tower	350.00			Notes Rec.	340.00
					Int. Income	10.00
2/20	Paul Smith	245.00	5.00	250.00		
2/28	Sundry Customers	110.00			Sales	110.00
	TOTALS	$1676.00	14.00	730.00		960.00

6

CASH DISBURSEMENTS

Date	Name	Net Cash	Purch. Disc.	Soc. Sec. Tax	With- hold. Taxes	Accts. Pay.	Miscellaneous Account	Amount
2/3	Sun Realty Co.	125					Rent	125
2/9	Bell Smith Co.	540	10			550		
2/10	First Nat'l Bank	808					{ Notes Pay.	800
							Int. Cost	8
2/14	James Roe Co.	1360	22			1382		
2/16	Roxy Desk Co.	125					Fur.&Fixt.	125
2/20	Baldwin Auto	1650					Del.Equip.	1650
2/28	Payroll	360		4	36		Sal.	400
2/28	A. New	215					A.New Pers.	215
	TOTALS	$5183	32	4	36	1932		3323

SALES BOOK

Date	Name	Accts. Rec.	Sales	Freight Out	Sales Tax
2/2	Booth & White	460.00	455.00	5.00	
2/10	Water & Co.	375.00	364.00	11.00	
2/14	Neville Bros.	204.00	200.00		4.00
2/26	A. Parker	918.00	900.00		18.00
	TOTALS	$1957.00	1919.00	16.00	22.00

PURCHASE BOOK

Date	Name	Accts. Payable	Purchases	Freight Inward	Miscellaneous Account	Amount
2/4	Walden Co.	800.00	800.00			
2/5	Power Telephone	17.00			Tel.	17.00
2/9	Mfgs. Ins. Co.	122.00			Insurance	122.00
2/12	Tower & Co.	756.00	748.00	8.00		
2/16	X-cel Express	13.00		13.00		
2/23	Braver & Co.	265.00	265.00			
2/28	Penn Stationers	65.00			Off. Supl.	65.00
	TOTALS	$2038.00	1813.00	21.00		204.00

Supply the balances of the following accounts on February 29, after all posting has been done for February. Put answers in the appropriate spaces on the right. (Give amounts only.)

1. Cash   1. ....
2. Notes Receivable   2. ....
3. Accounts Receivable   3. ....
4. Furniture and Fixtures   4. ....
5. Delivery Equipment   5. ....
6. Purchases   6. ....
7. Telephone   7. ....
8. Office Supplies   8. ....
9. Salaries   9. ....
10. Sales Discount   10. ....
11. Purchase Discount   11. ....
12. Insurance   12. ....
13. Freight Inward   13. ....
14. Sales   14. ....
15. Accounts Payable   15. ....
16. Freight Outward   16. ....

17. Notes Payable   17. ....
18. A. New, Capital   18. ....
19. A. New, Personal   19. ....
20. Sales Taxes Payable   20. ....
21. Withholding Taxes Payable   21. ....
22. Social Security Taxes Payable   22. ....
23. Interest Income   23. ....
24. Rent   24. ....
25. Interest Cost   25. ....

Questions 26-50.

DIRECTIONS:

Below is a list of some of the accounts containing balances in the ledger of the Ajax Company on December 31st after posting all entries for the year except adjusting and closing entries.

If the account *NORMALLY* would have a debit balance, write "D" in the proper numbered space on the right. If the amount *NORMALLY* would have a credit balance, write "C" in the proper numbered space on the right.

26. Notes Receivable   26. ....
27. Merchandise Inventory   27. ....
28. Notes Payable   28. ....
29. Interest on Notes Receivable   29. ....
30. Freight Inward   30. ....
31. Sales Discount   31. ....
32. Samuel Ajax Proprietor   32. ....
33. Purchase Returns and Allowances   33. ....
34. Land and Buildings   34. ....
35. Reserve for Depreciation of Furniture and Fixtures   35. ....
36. Purchase Discount   36. ....
37. Rent Collected from Sub-Tenants   37. ....
38. Taxes Accrued   38. ....
39. Notes Receivable Discounted   39. ....
40. Accounts Payable   40. ....
41. Interest on Notes Payable   41. ....
42. Sales Returns and Allowances   42. ....
43. Reserve for Bad Debts   43. ....
44. Income from Commissions   44. ....
45. Deposits from Customers on Containers   45. ....
46. Sales   46. ....
47. Accounts Receivable   47. ....
48. United States Government Bonds   48. ....
49. Sales Taxes Collected   49. ....
50. Deposit with Gas Company   50. ....

Questions 51-90

DIRECTIONS:

As an employee for Wallace and Pace, you have taken a trial balance of the general ledger on December 31. *After* posting all adjusting entries but *before* closing the accounts, you find your adjusted trial balance is correct. You are now requested to prepare a *CLASSIFIED* balance sheet using *only* the following classifications:

    A. Current Assets   B. Fixed Assets
    C. Deferred Charges   D. Current Liabilities
    E. Fixed Liabilities   F. Capital

Indicate the balance sheet classification of the following items by putting the letter (A to F) in the corresponding spaces on the right.

However, if any of the following items should *not* appear in your classified balance sheet, write the letter "P" in the corresponding space on the right.

51. Cash   51. ....
52. Furniture & Fixtures   52. ....
53. Notes Receivable   53. ....
54. Reserve for Bad Debts   54. ....
55. Merchandise Inventory 1/1   55. ....
56. Freight In   56. ....
57. A. Wallace, Capital   57. ....
58. Sales Returns   58. ....
59. Notes Payable   59. ....
60. Purchase Discount   60. ....
61. Reserve for Depreciation of Furniture & Fixtures   61. ....
62. Insurance Unexpired   62. ....
63. Interest Cost   63. ....
64. Salaries   64. ....
65. Shipping Supplies Inventory as of 12/31   65. ....
66. Accounts Receivable   66. ....
67. Bad Debts   67. ....
68. Shipping Supplies   68. ....
69. Mortgage Payable   69. ....
70. Depreciation on Furniture & Fixtures   70. ....
71. L. Pace, Personal (credit)   71. ....
72. Land, Buildings   72. ....
73. Depreciation on Buildings   73. ....
74. Interest Accrued on Notes Receivable   74. ....
75. Petty Cash Fund   75. ....
76. Taxes   76. ....
77. Sales Discount   77. ....
78. Merchandise Inventory 12/31   78. ....
79. Sales   79. ....
80. Interest Income   80. ....
81. Purchases   81. ....
82. Insurance   82. ....
83. Accounts Payable   83. ....
84. Salaries Accrued   84. ....
85. Reserve for Depreciation of Buildings   85. ....
86. Taxes Payable   86. ....
87. Purchase Returns   87. ....
88. Interest Accrued on Mortgage   88. ....
89. A. Wallace, Personal (debit)   89. ....
90. L. Pace, Capital   90. ....

Questions 91-110.

DIRECTIONS:

Below you will find a list of accounts with a number before each:

1. Accounts Payable   11. Petty Cash Fund
2. Accounts Receivable   12. Proprietor's Capital Account
3. Cash   13. Purchases
4. Freight Inward   14. Purchase Discounts
5. Freight Outward   15. Purchase Returns
6. Interest Cost   16. Real Estate
7. Interest Income   17. Sales
8. Notes Payable   18. Sales Discounts
9. Notes Receivable   19. Sales Returns
10. Notes Receivable Discounted   20. Selling Expenses

Using the number in front of each account, make journal entries for the transactions listed below.

DO NOT WRITE the names of the accounts in your answer space. Simply indicate in the proper space on the right, the numbers of the accounts to be debited or credited. *Always* give the number of the account to be debited *first*, *then* give the number of the account to be credited.

Example: If Cash is to be debited and Sales is to be credited, write as your answer 3-17.

91. Drew a check to establish a Petty Cash Fund. 91. ....
92. A. Paul, a customer, sent us a 60-day interest-bearing note for an invoice previously entered on our books. 92. ....
93. Sent a credit memorandum to a customer for goods returned to us. 93. ....
94. Our bank notified us that a customer's check was returned marked "insufficient funds." 94. ....
95. Accepted a 60-day draft drawn on us by a creditor for invoice previously entered on books. 95. ....
96. A customer sent us a check as a deposit on goods to be sent him. 96. ....
97. Issued a certified check for the purchase of real estate. 97. ....
98. Received notice from the bank that our account was charged for the payment of trade acceptance given to a creditor two months ago. 98. ....
99. Returned merchandise to a creditor and received a credit memorandum. 99. ....
100. Sent a check to a customer whose account had been overpaid in error. 100. ....
101. The proprietor invested additional cash in the business. 101. ....
102. Received a bank draft from a customer in payment of a note. 102. ....
103. Sent our 90-day interest bearing note to a creditor in settlement of account. 103. ....
104. Honored a sight draft drawn on us by one of our ceditors. 104. ....
105. Sold goods to a customer, terms 60 days. 105. ....
106. A customer's note, which we had discounted two months ago, was collected by our bank. 106. ....
107. Purchased merchandise, terms 2/10 E.O.M. 107. ....
108. Paid our note due today. 108. ....
109. A customer notifes us that he failed to deduct a discount on his last remittance. Sent him check for the discount. 109. ....
110. Last month's total of the Accounts Receivable column in the Cash Receipts book was posted in error to Notes Receivable Account. Make the correction entry. 110. ....

Questions 111-112.
DIRECTIONS:
Questions 111 and 112 are based on the following:
T. Lawson uses controlling accounts and a card system for the individual accounts with his customers and creditors.
The card containing the account with G. White, to whom he sells goods, has been lost. Reference to monthly schedules of Accounts Receivable shows that White owed $3500 on April 1; $2900 on May 1; and $4300 on June 1.
The cash book shows that Lawson received the following payments from White: $2500 on April 7; $3400 on April 14; and $3800 on May 25.
The journal shows that damaged goods were returned by White on April 15, $250, and that White received an allowance of $50 for shortages on May 16. White gave Lawson a note for $3200 on May 30.

10

111. What were the Sales to White during April?   111. ....
112. What were the Sales to White during May?   112. ....
Questions 113-114.
DIRECTIONS:

    Questions 113 and 114 are based on the following:

    Your cash book balance on July 31 was $9242.18.

    The bank statement sent to you on August 1 shows a credit for interest of $16.20 and a deduction of $4.50 for collection expenses.

    You discover that one check paid by the bank was made out for $78.29 and you had entered it in the cash book as $72.89.

    The checks outstanding are #235 for $409.08; #240 for $279.19; #241 for $42.10; and #247 for $913.56.

113. What balance did the bank report?   113. ....
114. What was your true cash balance on August 1?   114. ....
115. You received an invoice dated Sept. 5, terms 2/10, n/30,   115. ....
    f.o.b. destination, amounting to $350. The shipper paid
    $25 freight. On Sept. 8 you received a credit memorandum
    for $15 worth of goods returned.
    What was the amount of the check required to pay the invoice on Sept. 14?
116. On March 8 you drew a check to pay an invoice of $750,   116. ....
    terms 2/10, E.O.M., dated Feb. 3.
    What was the amount of the check?
117. On March 14 you drew a check to pay an invoice of $460,   117. ....
    which included $30 freight prepaid by shipper. Invoice
    dated March 6 carried items 5/10, n/60.
    What was the amount of the check?
118. March 15 - Your employer borrowed from his bank on his   118. ....
    own 90-day note for $1400. Rate of discount 6%.
    What amount should you enter in your net cash column in
    your cash receipts book?
119. May 9 - You discounted a customer's 60-day note at your   119. ....
    bank. Face of note was $480. Date of note was May 3rd.
    Discount rate was 6%.
    What was the amount of the net proceeds?
120. Your Dec. 31 trial balance contained an item for Inter-   120. ....
    est Income $165. On that date you discovered that you
    had collected $15 interest in advance, and that there was
    $22 interest accrued on customers' notes not yet due.
    What amount should be listed on the year's Profit and
    Loss Statement as Interest Income?

KEYS (CORRECT ANSWERS)

TEST 1

#	Answer	#	Answer
1.	C,E	41.	J;K
2.	F,H,I,K	42.	A;C,E
3.	B,D,E	43.	L;C
4.	None	44.	D;C
5.	F,K	45.	N;C
6.	G,K	46.	I,C;B
7.	F,K	47.	P;C
8.	A,E	48.	M;H
9.	F,K	49.	H;F
10.	B,E	50.	H;F
11.	A,E	51.	17900
12.	F,K	52.	P 1950
13.	None	53.	220
14.	A,D,E	54.	3565.71
15.	A,E	55.	11700
16.	F,K	56.	360
17.	None	57.	833.28
18.	F,K	58.	671.08
19.	None	59.	29400
20.	F,K	60.	208000
21.	B,E	61.	C
22.	A,E	62.	C
23.	G,J,K	63.	W
24.	None	64.	W
25.	F,K	65.	C
26.	C,E	66.	C
27.	A,E	67.	W
28.	B,D,F	68.	W
29.	B,D	69.	C
30.	None	70.	W
31.	C,E	71.	W
32.	C,D	72.	W
33.	None	73.	W
34.	B,F	74.	C
35.	C,D	75.	W
36.	F;C	76.	W
37.	A;K	77.	C
38.	A;O	78.	C
39.	J;K	79.	W
40.	K,G;C	80.	W

TEST 2

#	Answer	#	Answer	#	Answer
1.	4135	41.	D	81.	P
2.	2260	42.	D	82.	P
3.	4327	43.	C	83.	D
4.	875	44.	C	84.	D
5.	2850	45.	C	85.	B
6.	4663	46.	C	86.	D
7.	127	47.	D	87.	P
8.	445	48.	D	88.	D
9.	700	49.	C	89.	F
10.	94	50.	D	90.	F
11.	88	51.	A	91.	11-3
12.	282	52.	B	92.	9-2
13.	91	53.	A	93.	19-2
14.	5179	54.	A	94.	2-3
15.	2506	55.	P	95.	1-8
16.	24	56.	P	96.	3-2
17.	800	57.	F	97.	16-3
18.	12200	58.	P	98.	8-3
19.	95	59.	D	99.	1-15
20.	57	60.	P	100.	2-3
21.	64	61.	B	101.	3-12
22.	7	62.	A	102.	3-9
23.	10	63.	P	103.	1-8
24.	125	64.	P	104.	1-3
25.	8	65.	A	105.	2-17
26.	D	66.	A	106.	10-9
27.	D	67.	P	107.	13-1
28.	C	68.	P	108.	8-3
29.	C	69.	E	109.	18-3
30.	D	70.	P	110.	9-2
31.	D	71.	F	111.	5550
32.	C	72.	B	112.	8450
33.	C	73.	P	113.	10892.41
34.	D	74.	A	114.	9248.48
35.	C	75.	A	115.	328.30
36.	C	76.	P	116.	735
37.	C	77.	P	117.	438.50
38.	C	78.	A	118.	1379
39.	C	79.	P	119.	475.68
40.	C	80.	P	120.	172

BOOKKEEPING PROBLEMS
EXAMINATION SECTION
TEST 1

DIRECTIONS: Each question or incomplete statement is followed by several suggested answers or completions. Select the one that BEST answers the question or completes the statement. *PRINT THE LETTER OF THE CORRECT ANSWER IN THE SPACE AT THE RIGHT.*

1. The accounts in a general ledger are BEST arranged 1.____

    A. in numerical order
    B. according to the frequency with which each account is used
    C. according to the order in which the headings of the columns in the cash journals are arranged
    D. according to the order in which they are used in preparing financial statements

2. A physical inventory is an inventory obtained by 2.____

    A. an actual count of the items on hand
    B. adding the totals of the stock record cards
    C. deducting the cost of goods sold from the purchases for the period
    D. deducting the purchases from the sales for the period

3. Modern accounting practice favors the valuation of the inventories of a going concern at 3.____

    A. current market prices, if higher than cost
    B. cost or market, whichever is lower
    C. estimated selling price
    D. probable value at forced sale

4. A subsidiary ledger contains accounts which show 4.____

    A. details of contingent liabilities of undetermined amount
    B. totals of all asset accounts in the general ledger
    C. totals of all liability accounts in the general ledger
    D. details of an account in the general ledger

5. A statement of the assets, liabilities, and net worth of a business is called a 5.____

    A. trial balance   B. budget
    C. profit and loss statement   D. balance sheet

6. The one of the following which is NEVER properly considered a negotiable instrument is a(n) 6.____

    A. invoice   B. bond
    C. promissory note   D. endorsed check

7. The term *current assets* USUALLY includes such things as 7.____

    A. notes payable   B. machinery and equipment
    C. furniture and fixtures   D. accounts receivable

8. An accounting system which records revenues as soon as they are earned and records liabilities as soon as they are incurred regardless of the date of payment is said to operate on a(n) _____ basis.   8._____

    A. accrual   B. budgetary   C. encumbrance   D. cash

9. A *trial balance* is a list of   9._____

    A. the credit balances in all accounts in a general ledger
    B. all general ledger accounts and their balances
    C. the asset accounts in a general ledger and their balances
    D. the liability accounts in a general ledger and their balances

10. A controlling account contains the totals of   10._____

    A. the accounts used in preparing the balance sheet at the end of the fiscal period
    B. the individual amounts entered in the accounts of a subsidiary ledger during the fiscal period
    C. all entries in the general journal during the fiscal period
    D. the accounts used in preparing the profit and loss statement for the fiscal period

11. The ESSENTIAL nature of an asset is that it(s)   11._____

    A. must be tangible
    B. must be easily converted into cash
    C. must have value
    D. cost must be included in the profit and loss statement

12. When an asset is depreciated on the straight-line basis, the amount charged off for depreciation   12._____

    A. is greater in the earlier years of the asset's life
    B. is greater in the later years of the asset's life
    C. varies each year according to the extent to which the asset is used during the year
    D. is equal each full year of the asset's life

Questions 13-27.

DIRECTIONS: Questions 13 to 27 consist of a list of some of the accounts in a general ledger. Indicate whether each account listed generally contains a debit or a credit balance by putting the letter D (for debit balance) or the letter C (for credit balance) in the correspondingly numbered space on the right for each account listed. For example, for the account Cash, which generally contains a debit balance, you would give the letter D as your answer.

13. Sales Taxes Collected   13._____

14. Social Security Taxes Paid by Employer   14._____

15. Deposits from Customers   15._____

16. Freight Inward   16._____

17. Sales Discount   17._____

18. Withholding Taxes Payable   18.____

19. L. Norton, Drawings   19.____

20. Office Salaries   20.____

21. Merchandise Inventory   21.____

22. L. Norton, Capital   22.____

23. Purchases Returns   23.____

24. Unearned Rent Income   24.____

25. Reserve for Bad Debts   25.____

26. Depreciation of Machinery   26.____

27. Insurance Prepaid   27.____

Questions 28-42.

DIRECTIONS: Questions 28 to 42 consist of a list of some of the accounts in a general ledger. For the purpose of preparing financial statements, each of these accounts is to be classified into one of the following five major classifications, lettered A to E, as follows:
A. Assets   B. Liabilities   C. Proprietorship
D. Income   E. Expense
You are to indicate the classification to which each account belongs by printing the correct letter, A, B, C, D, or E, in the correspondingly numbered space on the right. For example, for the account Furniture and Fixtures, which is an asset account, you would print the letter A.

28. Notes Receivable   28.____

29. Sales   29.____

30. Wages Payable   30.____

31. Office Salaries   31.____

32. Capital Stock Authorized   32.____

33. Goodwill   33.____

34. Capital Surplus   34.____

35. Office Supplies Used   35.____

36. Interest Payable   36.____

37. Prepaid Rent   37.____

38. Interest Cost   38.____

39. Accounts Payable   39.____

40. Prepaid Insurance   40.____

41. Merchandise Inventory   41.____

42. Interest Earned   42.____

43. A trial balance will NOT indicate that an error has been made in   43.____

    A. computing the balance of an account
    B. entering an amount in the wrong account
    C. carrying forward the balance of an account
    D. entering an amount on the wrong side of an account

44. Many business firms maintain a book of original entry in which all bills to be paid are   44.____
recorded.
This book is known as a

    A. purchase returns journal   B. subsidiary ledger
    C. voucher register   D. notes payable register

45. Many business firms provide a petty cash fund from which to pay for small items in order   45.____
to avoid the issuing of many small checks.
If this fund is replenished periodically to restore it to its original amount, the fund is called
a(n) _____ fund.

    A. imprest   B. debenture
    C. adjustment   D. expense reserve

46. A firm which voluntarily terminates business, selling its assets and paying its liabilities, is   46.____
said to be in

    A. receivership   B. liquidation
    C. depletion   D. amortization

47. The phrase *3%-10 days* on an invoice ORDINARILY means that   47.____

    A. 3% of the amount must be paid each 10 days
    B. the purchaser is entitled to only ten days credit
    C. a discount of 3% will be allowed for payment in 10 days
    D. the entire amount must be paid in 10 days or a penalty of 3% of the amount due
       will be added

48. The CHIEF disadvantage of *single-entry* bookkeeping is that it   48.____

    A. is too difficult to operate
    B. is illegal for income tax purposes
    C. provides no possibility of determining net profits
    D. furnishes an incomplete picture of the business

49. Sales *minus* cost of goods sold *equals*   49.____

    A. net profit   B. gross sales
    C. gross profit   D. net sales

50. The amounts of the transactions recorded in a journal are transferred to the general led-   50._____
    ger accounts by a process known as

    A.   auditing   B.   balancing   C.   posting   D.   verifying

51. A merchant purchased a stock of goods and priced these goods so as to gain 40% on   51._____
    the cost to him.
    If the merchant sold these goods for $840, the COST of these goods to him was

    A. $556   B. $600   C. $348   D. $925

52. In the interest at 6% for one full year on a principal sum amounts to $12, the *principal*   52._____
    sum is

    A. $150   B. $96   C. $196   D. $200

53. On October 17, a business man discounted a customer's 90-day non-interest bearing   53._____
    note at his bank. The face of the note was $960, and it was dated September 28. The
    discount rate was 5%.
    Using a 360-day year, the amount in cash that the business man received from the bank
    was MOST NEARLY

    A. $899.33   B. $950.67   C. $967.50   D. $989.75

54. A certain correctly totaled cash receipts journal contained the following columns: Net   54._____
    Cash Debit, Accounts Receivable, Sales Discounts, and General.
    At the end of April, the totals of the columns were as follows: Net Cash Debit -
    $18,925.15, Accounts Receivable (not given), Sales Discounts - $379.65, General -
    $5,639.25.
    The TOTAL of the Accounts Receivable column was

    A. $11,194.50   B. $21,344.32   C. $7,621.19   D. $13,665.55

55. In its first year of operation, a retail store had cash sales of $49,000 and installment sales   55._____
    of $41,000.
    If 12% of the amount of these installment sales were collected in that year, the TOTAL
    amount of cash received from sales was

    A. $22,176   B. $34,987   C. $53,920   D. $55,650

56. I. Conklin and J. Ulster formed a partnership and agreed to share profits in proportion to   56._____
    their initial capital investments. I. Conklin invested $15,000 and J. Ulster invested
    $12,500.
    If the profits for the year were $16,500, J. Ulster's share of the profits was

    A. $6,750   B. $7,500   C. $8,100   D. $8,300

57. In a certain city, the tax rate on real estate one year was $48.75 per thousand dollars of   57._____
    assessed valuation. If an apartment house in that city was assessed for $185,000, the
    real estate tax payable by the owner of that house was MOST NEARLY

    A. $9,018.75   B. $9,009.75   C. $8,900.00   D. $8,905.25

58. A correctly totaled cash payments journal contained the following columns: Net Cash, Accounts Payable, Purchase Discounts, General.
At the end of April, the totals of the columns were as follows: Net Cash - $18,375.60, Accounts Payable - $16,981.19, Purchase Discounts (not given), General - $1,875.37.
The TOTAL of the Purchase Discounts column was

   A. $120.36   B. $239.87   C. $480.96   D. $670.51

58.____

59. On January 1, the credit balance of the Accounts Payable account in a general ledger was $9,139.87. For the month of January, the Purchase Journal total amounted to $3,467.81; the Accounts Payable column in the Cash Disbursements Journal amounted to $2,935.55; the total of the Returned Purchases Journal for January amounted to $173.15; and the Miscellaneous column in the Cash Disbursements Journal showed that $750 had been paid in January on notes given to creditors and entered in previous months.
The BALANCE in the Accounts Payable account at the end of January was

   A. $8,437.89   B. $9,498.98   C. $9,998.98   D. $10,132.68

59.____

60. The bank statement received from his bank by a business man showed a certain balance for the month of June. This bank statement showed a service charge of $5.19 for the month. He discovered that a check drawn by him in the amount of $83.75 and returned by the bank had been entered on the stub of his checkbook as $38.75. He also found that two checks which he had issued, #29 for $37.18 and #33 for $18.69, were not listed on the statement and had not been returned by the bank. The balance in his checkbook before he reconciled it with the balance shown on the bank statement was $8,917.91.
The BALANCE on the bank statement was

   A. $8,903.97   B. $8,923.59   C. $8,997.65   D. $9,303.95

60.____

———

KEY (CORRECT ANSWERS)

1.	D	16.	D	31.	E	46.	B
2.	A	17.	D	32.	C	47.	C
3.	B	18.	C	33.	A	48.	D
4.	D	19.	D	34.	C	49.	C
5.	D	20.	D	35.	E	50.	C
6.	A	21.	D	36.	B	51.	B
7.	D	22.	C	37.	A	52.	D
8.	A	23.	C	38.	E	53.	B
9.	B	24.	C	39.	B	54.	D
10.	B	25.	C	40.	A	55.	C
11.	C	26.	D	41.	A	56.	B
12.	D	27.	D	42.	D	57.	A
13.	C	28.	A	43.	B	58.	C
14.	D	29.	D	44.	C	59.	B
15.	C	30.	B	45.	A	60.	B

TEST 2

Questions 1-25.

DIRECTIONS:
1. Below you will find the general ledger balances on February 28 in the books of C. Dutton.
2. On the following pages, you will find all the entries on the books of C. Dutton for the month of March.
3. In the appropriate spaces on the right, you are to supply the new balances for the accounts called for at the end of March.

The correct balances in the general ledger of C. Dutton on February 28 were as follows: (NOTE: The accounts below have not been arranged in the customary trial balance form.)

Cash	$4,336
Accounts Receivable	8,165
Notes Receivable	2,200
Furniture and Fixtures	9,000
Merchandise Inventory 1/1	4,175
Accounts Payable	5,560
Notes Payable	1,500
Reserve for Depreciation of Furniture and Fixtures	1,800
C. Dutton, Capital	14,162
C. Dutton, Drawing	900
Purchases	42,600
Freight In	36
Rent	1,750
Light	126
Telephone	63
Salaries	4,076
Shipping Expenses	368
Sales	53,200
Sales Biscount	637
Purchase Biscount	596
City Sales Tax Collected	804
Social Security Taxes Payable	96
Withholding Taxes Payable	714

CASH RECEIPTS

Date	Name	Net Cash	Accounts Receivable	Sales Disc.	Miscellaneous Acct.	Amount
3/1	T. Blint	6,027.00	6,150.00	123.00		
	K . Crowe	1,015.00			Notes Rec.	1,000.00
					Int. Income	15.00
3/10	N. Tandy	3,969.00	4,050.00	81.00		
3/17	Rebuilt Desk Co.	45.00			Furn. & Fixt.	45.00
3/24	J. Walter	2,910.00	3,000.00	90.00		
3/31	National Federal Bank	3,000.00			Notes Payable	3,000.00
		16,966.00	13,200.00	294.00		4,060.00

CASH DISBURSEMENTS

Date		Net Cash	Accts. Pay.	Purch Disc.	Soc. Sec. Tax	With-hold Tax	Miscellaneous Acct.	Amount
3/1	Bliss Realty Co.	875.00					Rent	875.00
3/4	Con. Edison	54.00					Light	54.00
3/10	D. LaRue	2,891.00	2,950.00	59.00				
3/15	Payroll	747.00			26.00	175.	Sal.	948.00
3/19	Rebuilt Desk Co.	115.00					Furn/Fixt	115.00
3/26	Jiggs & Co.	3,686.00	3,800.00	114.00				
3/30	Nat'l Fed Bank	1,218.00					Notes Pay.	1200.00
							Int. Cost	18.00
3/31	Payroll	733.00			22.00	171.	Salary	926.00
3/31	C. Dutton	600.00					Draw	600.00
		10,919.00	6,750.00	173.00	48.00	346.00		4736.00

SALES BOOK

Date	Name	Accts. Rec.	Sales	City Sales Tax
3/3	K . Crowe	6,850.00	6,665.00	185.00
3/10	J. Walters	5,730.00	5,730.00	
3/16	N. Tandy	3,100.00	3,007.00	93.00
3/25	Willis & Co.	7,278.00	7,069.00	209.00
3/30	V. Clyburne	2,190.00	2,190.00	
		25,148.00	24,661.00	487.00

PURCHASE BOOK

Date		Accts. Pay.	Purchases	Freight In	Miscellaneous Acct.	Amount
3/4	Jiggs & Co.	5,212.00	5,070.00	142.00		
3/11	Barton & Co.	320.00			Ins. Prepd.	320.00
3/16	A. Field	6,368.00	6,179.00	189.00		
3/19	Smith Delivery	22.00			Ship. Exp.	22.00
3/23	N.Y. Telephone	29.00			Telephone	29.00
3/26	D . LaRue	3,000.00	3,000.00			
3/29	App & App	7,531.00	7,168.00	363.00		
		22,482.00	21,417.00	694.00		371.00

Supply the balances of the following accounts on March 31 after all posting has been done for March. Put answers in the appropriate spaces on the right. Give amounts only.

1. Cash   1.____

2. Accounts Receivable   2.____

3. Notes Receivable   3.____

4. Insurance Prepaid   4.____

5. Furniture and Fixtures   5.____

6. Accounts Payable   6.____

7. Notes Payable   7.____

8.	Reserve for Depreciation of Furniture and Fixtures	8._____
9.	C. Dutton, Capital	9._____
10.	C. Dutton, Drawing	10._____
11.	Purchases	11._____
12.	Freight In	12._____
13.	Rent	13._____
14.	Light	14._____
15.	Telephone	15._____
16.	Salaries	16._____
17.	Shipping Expenses	17._____
18.	Sales	18._____
19.	Sales Discount	19._____
20.	Purchase Discount	20._____
21.	City Sales Tax Collected	21._____
22.	Social Security Taxes Payable	22._____
23.	Withholding Taxes Payable	23._____
24.	Interest Income	24._____
25.	Interest Cost	25._____

Questions 26-35.

DIRECTIONS: Mr. Adams has a complete set of books - Cash Journals, Purchase and Sales Journals, and a General Journal. Below you will find the General Journal used by Mr. Adams. Under the heading of each money column, you will find a letter of the alphabet. Following the General Journal, there is a series of transactions. You are to determine the correct entry for each transaction and then show on the right in the appropriate space the columns to be used. For example, if a certain transaction results in an entry of $100 in the Notes Receiving Column (on the left side) and an entry of $100 in the General Ledger Column (on the right side), in the appropriate space on the right, you should write A, D. If the record of the transaction requires the use of more than two columns, your answer should contain more than two letters. DO NOT PUT THE AMOUNTS IN YOUR ANSWER SPACE. The LETTERS of the columns to be used are sufficient. If a transaction requires no entry in the General Journal, write *None* in the appropriate space in your answer space, even though a record would be made in some other journal.

GENERAL JOURNAL

Notes Receivable	Accounts Payable	General Ledger	L. F.		General Ledger	Accounts Receivable	Notes Payable
A	B	C			D	E	F

26. We sent Tripp & Co. a 30-day trade acceptance for $500 for merchandise sold him today. They accepted it. 26.____

27. The proprietor, Mr. Adams, returned $100 in cash to be deposited, representing Traveling Expenses he had not used. 27.____

28. An entry in the purchase journal last month for a purchase invoice from V. Valides for $647 was erroneously entered in the purchase journal as $746 and posted as such. 28.____

29. A check for $200 received from Mr. Breen was erroneously credited to account of P. Ungar. 29.____

30. In posting the totals of the cash receipts journal last month, an item of bank discount of $30 on our note for $1500 discounted for 60 days was included in the total posted to the sales discount account. 30.____

31. M. Hogan paid his note of $600 and interest of $12 and his account was credited for $612. 31.____

32. Mr. Blow informed us he could not pay his invoice of $2000 due today. Instead, he sent us his 30-day note for $2000 for 30 days bearing interest at 6% per annum. 32.____

33. The proprietor, Mr. Adams, drew $75 to buy his daughter a U.S. Bond. 33.____

34. Mr. O'Brien wrote to us that we overcharged him on an invoice last week. 34.____

35. Returned $120 worth of merchandise to Pecora & Co. and received their credit memorandum. 35.____

Questions 36-50.

DIRECTIONS: In Questions 36 to 50, you will find a list of accounts with a number before each.

1. Cash
2. Accounts Receivable
3. Notes Receivable
4. Notes Receivable Discounted
5. Furniture and Fixtures
6. Delivery Equipment
7. Insurance Prepaid
8. Depreciation on Delivery Equipment
9. Bad Debts
10. Purchases
11. Discount on Purchases
12. Sales

13. Discount on Sales
14. Accounts Payable
15. Notes Payable
16. Interest Cost
17. Reserve for Depreciation on Delivery Equipment
18. Reserve for Bad Debts
19. Sales Taxes Collected
20. Ben Miller, Capital
21. Ben Miller, Drawing
22. Interest Income
23. Purchase Returns

Using the number in front of each account title (using no accounts not listed), make journal entries for the transactions given below. Do not write the names of the accounts in your answer space. Simply indicate in the proper space on the right the numbers of the accounts to be debited or credited. Always give the number or numbers of the accounts to be debited first, then give the number or numbers of accounts to be credited. For example, if furniture and fixtures and delivery equipment are to be debited, and cash and notes payable are to be credited in a certain transaction, then write in your answer space 5, 6 - 1, 15 (use a dash to separate the debits from the credits).

36. F. Pierce, a customer, went into bankruptcy owing us $600. We received a check for $200.

36._____

37. Later in the month, we are informed that there is no possibility of collecting the balance from F. Pierce. There is a sufficient balance in the Reserve for Bad Debts to take care of the above.

37._____

38. Set up the Depreciation on the Delivery Equipment for the year amounting to $240.

38._____

39. Discounted M. Colby's note for $500 today and received $490 in proceeds.

39._____

40. Mr. Miller, the proprietor, invested $2000 in the business.

40._____

41. Paid our note due to Dillon & Co. today for $800 with interest of $16.

41._____

42. Accepted Finnegan's trade acceptance for $1500 for merchandise bought today.

42._____

43. Create a Reserve for Bad Debts of $2000 at the end of the year.

43._____

44. Returned to Dillon & Co. $30 worth of damaged merchandise for credit. They allowed it.

44._____

45. G. Garry claimed a discount of $12 which we had failed to allow him. He had already paid his bill. Sent him check for $12.

45._____

46. On one sale during the month, we had failed to collect the Sales Tax of $15. Wrote to the customer and he sent us a check for $15.

46._____

47. M. Colby paid his note due today which we had discounted two months ago.

47._____

48. Bought a new safe for $875 from Cramer & Co., terms 2/10, n/60 days. Agreed to pay them in 60 days.

48._____

49. Bought merchandise during the month amounting to $17,500 - all on account.

49._____

50. On December 31, paid for a Fire Insurance policy to run for three years from that date - premium was $480.

50._____

51. The following information was taken from the ledger of Peter Dolan on Dec. 31 after adjusting entries had been posted to the ledger.

51._____

Sales Income	$60,000
Sales Returns	3,500
Mdse. Purchases	42,000
Inventory of 1/1	9,400
Sales Taxes Payable	360
Freight Inward	225
Inventory 12/31	7,640
Insurance Unexpired	163

Find the gross profit on Sales for the year.

52. On March 31, your bank sent you a statement of account. You compared the canceled   52._____
checks with the stubs in your checkbook and found the following:

    Check #34 - $56.00 had not been paid by the bank

            #44 - $38.00 had been paid by the bank as $38.89 because the amount
on the check did not agree with your stub in the checkbook

            #52 - $76.50 had not been returned by the bank, though the check had
been certified

            #57 - $127.42 had not been paid by the bank

What total amount would you deduct from the balance on the bank's statement as
checks outstanding?

53. On April 30, Mr. Jolley received his statement of account from the bank. A comparison of   53._____
the bank statement and your checkbook revealed the following: Checkbook balance
$5,640; this included a deposit of $325 on the last day of April which had not been
entered on the bank statement.

You also find the following:

    Check #69 - $89.00 had not been paid by the bank

            #70 - Paid by the bank as $47.55, had been entered in your checkbook
as $45.57

            #76 - $114.30 had not been paid by the bank

The bank statement included a debit memo of $4.00 for excessive activity during the
month.

What was the balance on the bank statement?

54. An invoice dated January 15 for merchandise you bought added up to $876.00. The   54._____
terms were 3/10, n/60, F.O.B. DESTINATION. When the goods arrived, you paid freight
amounting to $8.50. On January 20, you returned goods billed at $26 and received credit
therefor. You paid the bill on January 24.

What was the amount of your check?

55. Income taxes paid by residents of a certain state are based on the balance of taxable   55._____
income at the following

    rates: 2% on first $1000 or less

               3% on 2nd and 3rd $1000

               4% on 4th and 5th $1000

               5% on 6th and 7th $1000

               6% on 8th and 9th $1000

               7% on all   over $9000

What would be the NORMAL income tax to be paid by a resident of that state whose
taxable balance of income was $6,750?

56. A salesman's gross earnings for the year came to $8,820. His rate of Commission was   56._____
5% of his sales to customers after deducting returns by customers. During the year, his
customers returned 10% of the goods they purchased. What were his total sales during
the year before deducting returns?

57. On December 31, the insurance account contained a debit for $144 for a three-year fire   57._____
insurance policy dated August 1. What amount should be listed on the balance sheet of
December 31 of that year?

58. A partnership began business on January 1 with partners' investments of $26,000. Dur-   58.____
    ing the year, the partners drew $18,500 for personal use. On December 31, the assets of
    the firm were $46,300, and the liabilities were $15,600. What was the firm's net profit for
    the year? (Write P or L before your answer.)

59. The rent income account of a real estate firm showed a total balance of $75,640 at the   59.____
    end of 1986. Of this amount, $3,545 represented prepaid 1987 rents. The account also
    included entries for 1986 rents due from tenants but not yet collected, amounting to
    $2,400.
    What amount should be listed on the profit and loss statement as rent income for
    1986?

60. You discounted a customer's note for $7,200 at your bank at the rate of 6% and received   60.____
    net proceeds of $7,182.
    How many days did the note have to run from date of discount to date of maturity?
    (Use 360 days to the year.)

Questions 61-90.

DIRECTIONS: In Questions 61 to 90, you will find a list of ledger accounts. Indicate whether
             an account is generally listed in the Trial Balance as a DEBIT or as a CREDIT
             by putting the letter D or the letter C in the correct space on the right for each
             account listed.

61. Sales   61.____

62. Land   62.____

63. Notes Payable   63.____

64. Traveling Expenses   64.____

65. Purchases   65.____

66. Buildings   66.____

67. Merchandise Inventory   67.____

68. Machinery and Equipment   68.____

69. Notes Receivable   69.____

70. Bonds Payable   70.____

71. Advertising   71.____

72. Delivery Expense   72.____

73. Cash   73.____

74.   Accounts Payable   74._____

75.   Interest on Bonds   75._____

76.   Real Estate Taxes   76._____

77.   Accounts Receivable   77._____

78.   Don Burch, Proprietor   78._____

79.   Sales Discount   79._____

80.   Withholding Taxes   80._____

81.   Depreciation   81._____

82.   Prepaid Insurance   82._____

83.   Reserve for Dep. on Buildings   83._____

84.   Rent Income   84._____

85.   Reserve for Bad Debts   85._____

86.   Don Burch, Drawing Account   86._____

87.   Sales Returns   87._____

88.   Bad Debts   88._____

89.   Purchase Discount   89._____

90.   Reserve for Dep. on Machinery & Equipment   90._____

———

KEY (CORRECT ANSWERS)

1.	$ 10,383	31.	C,D,D	61.	C
2.	$ 20,113	32.	A,E	62.	D
3.	$ 1,200	33.	None	63.	C
4.	$ 320	34.	C,E	64.	D
5.	$ 9,070	35.	B,D	65.	D
6.	$ 21,292	36.	1-2	66.	D
7.	$ 3,300	37.	18-2	67.	D
8.	$ 1,800	38.	8-17	68.	D
9.	$ 14,162	39.	1,16-4	69.	D
10.	$ 1,500	40.	1-20	70.	C
11.	$ 64,017	41.	15,16-1	71.	D
12.	$ 730	42.	14-15	72.	D
13.	$ 2,625	43.	9-18	73.	D
14.	$ 180	44.	14-23	74.	C
15.	$ 92	45.	13-1	75.	D
16.	$ 5,950	46.	1-19	76.	D
17.	$ 390	47.	4-3	77.	D
18.	$ 77,861	48.	5-14	78.	C
19.	$ 931	49.	10-14	79.	D
20.	$ 769	50.	7-1	80.	C
21.	$ 1,291	51.	$12,515	81.	D
22.	$ 144	52.	$ 183.42	82.	D
23.	$ 1,060	53.	$ 5,512.32	83.	C
24.	$ 15	54.	$ 816	84.	C
25.	$ 18	55.	$ 247.50	85.	C
26.	A-E	56.	$196,000	86.	D
27.	None	57.	$ 124	87.	D
28.	B-D	58.	P $23,200	88.	D
29.	C,E	59.	$72,095	89.	C
30.	C,D	60.	15	90.	C

TEST 3

DIRECTIONS: Each question or incomplete statement is followed by several suggested answers or completions. Select the one that BEST answers the question or completes the statement. *PRINT THE LETTER OF THE CORRECT ANSWER IN THE SPACE AT THE RIGHT.*

1. Of the following taxes, the one which is levied MOST NEARLY in accordance with ability to pay is a(n) _____ tax.   1._____

   A. excise   B. income
   C. general property   D. sales

2. When a check has been lost, the bank on which it is drawn should ORDINARILY be notified and instructed to   2._____

   A. stop payment on the check
   B. issue a duplicate of the check
   C. charge the account of the drawer for the amount of the check
   D. certify the check

3. The profit and loss statement prepared for a retail store does NOT ordinarily show   3._____

   A. the cost of goods sold
   B. depreciation of fixtures and equipment
   C. expenditures for salaries of employees
   D. the net worth of the proprietor

4. When two business corporations join their assets and liabilities to form a new corporation, the procedures is called a(n)   4._____

   A. merger   B. liquidation
   C. receivership   D. exchange

5. The method of depreciation which deducts an equal amount each full year of an asset's life is called _____ depreciation.   5._____

   A. sum-of-years digits   B. declining balance
   C. straight-line   D. service-hours

6. A fixed asset is an asset that   6._____

   A. is held primarily for sale to customers
   B. is used in the conduct of the business until worn out or replaced
   C. is readily convertible into cash
   D. has no definite value

7. The gross profit on sales for a period is determined by   7._____

   A. subtracting the cost of goods sold from the sales
   B. subtracting the sales returns and the discounts on sales from the gross sales
   C. subtracting the sales from the purchases for the period
   D. finding the difference between the inventory of merchandise at the beginning of the period and the inventory of merchandise at the end of the period

8. The term *auditing* refers to the   8._____

    A. entering of amounts from the journals into the general ledger
    B. reconciliation of the accounts in a subsidiary ledger with the controlling account in the general ledger
    C. preparation of a trial balance of the accounts in the general ledger
    D. examination of the general ledger and other records of a concern to determine its true financial condition

9. A voucher register is a   9._____

    A. type of electric cash register
    B. list of customers whose accounts are past due
    C. list of the assets of a business
    D. book in which bills to be paid are recorded

10. The account DISCOUNT ON PURCHASES is *properly* closed directly to the _____ account.   10._____

    A. Accounts Payable   B. Sales
    C. Purchases   D. Fixtures

11. The account UNEARNED RENTAL INCOME is *usually* considered a(n) _____ account.   11._____

    A. asset   B. nominal   C. capital   D. liability

12. A controlling account is an account which contains   12._____

    A. the totals of *all* the expense accounts in the general ledger
    B. the total of the amounts entered in the accounts in a subsidiary ledger
    C. the total of the depreciation on fixtures claimed in *all* preceding years
    D. *all* totals of the income and expense accounts before closing to the Profit and Loss account

13. The purpose of the DRAWING account in the general ledger of an individual enterprise is to show the   13._____

    A. salaries paid to the employees
    B. amounts paid to independent contractors for services rendered
    C. amounts taken by the proprietor for his personal use
    D. total of payments made for general expenses of the business

14. The phrase *2%/10 net 30 days* on an invoice ORDINARILY means that   14._____

    A. 2% of the amount must be paid within 30 days
    B. the purchaser must add 2% to the amount of the invoice if he fails to pay within 30 days
    C. the entire amount must be paid within 30 days
    D. the purchaser may deduct 2% from the amount if he pays within 30 days

15. The ESSENTIAL characteristic of a C.O.D. sale of merchandise is that the   15._____

    A. purchaser pays for the merchandise upon its receipt by him
    B. seller guarantees the merchandise to be as specified by him
    C. merchandise is delivered by a common carrier
    D. purchaser is permitted to pay for the merchandise in convenient installments

16. If the drawer of a check makes an error in writing the amount of the check, he should   16.____

    A.   erase the error and insert the correct amount
    B.   cross out the error and insert the correct amount
    C.   destroy the check and prepare another one
    D.   write the correct amount directly above the incorrect one

17. States do NOT levy a(n) _____ tax.   17.____

    A.   unemployment insurance   B.   income
    C.   corporation franchise   D.   export

18. The cost of goods sold by a retail store is PROPERLY determined by   18.____

    A.   *adding* the closing inventory to the total of the opening inventory and the pur-
        chases for the year
    B.   *deducting* the closing inventory from the total of the opening inventory and the pur-
        chases for the year
    C.   *deducting* the total of the opening and closing inventories from the purchases for
        the year
    D.   *adding* the total of the opening and closing inventories

19. The PRIMARY purpose of a trial balance is to determine   19.____

    A.   that all transactions have been entered in the journals
    B.   the accuracy of the totals in the general ledger
    C.   the correctness of the amounts entered in the journals
    D.   that amounts have been posted to the proper accounts in the general ledger

20. The SURPLUS account of a corporation is *ordinarily* used to record   20.____

    A.   the actual amount subscribed by stockholders
    B.   the amount of profits earned by the corporation
    C.   any excess of current assets over current liabilities
    D.   the total of the fixed assets of the corporation

Questions 21-30.

DIRECTIONS: Each of Questions 21 to 30 consists of a typical transaction of Our Business
                followed by the debit and credit (amounts omitted) of the journal entry for that
                transaction. For each of these questions, the debit and credit given may be
                appropriately classified under one of the following categories:

    A.   The debit of the journal entry is CORRECT but the credit is INCORRECT.
    B.   The debit of the journal entry is INCORRECT but the credit is CORRECT.
    C.   BOTH the debit and the credit of the journal entry are correct.
    D.   BOTH the debit and the credit of the journal entry are incorrect.

Examine each question carefully. Then, in the correspondingly numbered space on the
right, mark as your answer the letter preceding the category which is the BEST of the
four suggested above.

SAMPLE QUESTION: We purchased a desk for cash.
Debit: Office Equipment
Credit: Accounts Payable

In this example, the debit is correct but the credit is incorrect. Therefore, you should mark A as your answer.

21. We sent a check for $500 to R. Thomas in payment for an invoice for that amount.
Debit: Cash   Credit: Accounts Receivable   21._____

22. We took merchandise, amounting to $35, for our own use.
Debit: Proprietor, Personal   Credit: Purchases   22._____

23. Arthur Townsend's 90-day note for $350, which was discounted by us at our bank last month, was paid by him today.   23._____
Debit: Notes Receivable Discounted
Credit: Accounts Receivable

24. We sold merchandise to T. Wilson on account of $275.   24._____
Debit: Accounts Payable   Credit: Sales

25. We returned damaged merchandise to B. Lowell and received a credit memorandum from him for $28.   25._____
Debit: Accounts Payable
Credit: Sales Returns and Allowances

26. We paid our 30-day note given to Mr. Kane for $650 without interest.   26._____
Debit: Notes Receivable   Credit: Cash

27. We sent Chet Carr a check for $10.50 for a discount he had forgotten to take when he paid us for merchandise this week.   27._____
Debit: Sales Discounts   Credit: Cash

28. The bank loaned us $1000, and we invested it in the business.   28._____
Debit: Cash   Credit: Loan Receivable

29. We recorded depreciation for the year on our office equipment.   29._____
Debit: Reserve for Depreciation of Office Equipment
Credit: Depreciation of Office Equipment

30. One of our customers, Allen Koren, was declared bankrupt and his debt of $25 to us was canceled.   30._____
Debit: Reserve for Bad Debts Credit: Accounts Receivable

Questions 31-45.

DIRECTIONS: Questions 31 to 45 consist of a list of some of the accounts in the general ledger of a corporation which operates a retail store. Indicate whether each account listed contains generally a debit or credit balance by marking the letter D (for debit balance) or the letter C (for credit balance) in the correspondingly numbered space on the right.
For example, for the account Cash, which generally contains a debit balance, you would mark the letter D as your answer.

31. Rent Expense   31._____

32. Allowance for Depreciation of Fixtures   32._____

33. Sales Returns and Allowances   33._____

34. Security Deposit for Electricity   34._____

35. Accrued Salaries Payable   35._____

36. Dividends Payable   36._____

37. Petty Cash Fund   37._____

38. Notes Receivable Discounted   38._____

39. Surplus   39._____

40. Capital Stock Authorized   40._____

41. Insurance Expense   41._____

42. Sales for Cash   42._____

43. Purchase Discounts   43._____

44. Automobile Delivery Equipment   44._____

45. Bad Debts Expense   45._____

Questions 46-60.

DIRECTIONS: Questions 46 to 60 consist of a list of some of the accounts in a general ledger. For the purpose of preparing financial statements, each of these accounts is to be classified into one of the following five major classifications, lettered A to E, as follows:
A. Assets B. Liabilities C. Income D. Expense E. Capital You are to indicate the classification to which each belongs by marking the appropriate letter, A, B, C, D or E. in the correspondingly numbered space on the right. For example, for the account MERCHANDISE INVENTORY, which is an asset account, you would mark the letter A as your answer.

46. Purchases   46._____

47. Prepaid Interest   47._____

48. Cash in Bank   48._____

49. Depreciation of Fixtures   49._____

50. Accounts Receivable   50.____

51. Mortgage Payable   51.____

52. Accrued Interest Receivable   52.____

53. Bad Debts   53.____

54. Insurance Expired   54.____

55. Treasury Stock   55.____

56. Investments   56.____

57. Loan to Partner   57.____

58. Unearned Rent Received   58.____

59. Petty Cash Fund   59.____

60. Loss on Sale of Equipment   60.____

KEY (CORRECT ANSWERS)

1.	B	16.	C	31.	D	46.	D
2.	A	17.	D	32.	C	47.	A
3.	D	18.	B	33.	D	48.	A
4.	A	19.	B	34.	D	49.	D
5.	C	20.	B	35.	C	50.	A
6.	B	21.	D	36.	C	51.	B
7.	A	22.	C	37.	D	52.	A
8.	D	23.	A	38.	C	53.	D
9.	D	24.	B	39.	C	54.	D
10.	C	25.	A	40.	C	55.	E
11.	D	26.	B	41.	D	56.	A
12.	B	27.	C	42.	C	57.	A
13.	C	28.	A	43.	C	58.	B
14.	C	29.	D	44.	D	59.	A
15.	A	30.	C	45.	D	60.	D

EXAMINATION SECTION
TEST 1

DIRECTIONS: Directly and concisely, using brief answer form, answer the following questions.

1.   On what side of the balance sheet do notes receivable appear?

2.   What two classes of accounts are generally kept in a subsidiary ledger?

3.   What account should you credit when the firm discounts a non-interest-bearing note of a customer at a bank?

4.   What does total cost of stock minus inventory at the end equal?

5.   _____ is a personal account with the credit side larger than the debit side.

6.   What are material goods, claims, and property rights as applied to business called?

7.   What is indicated if the interest account is debited?

8.   What are allowances made in the books to offset shrinkage in asset accounts called?

9.   What is the fund called which is established for the redemption of bonds or other obligations?

10.   What is the book of final entry called?

———

KEY (CORRECT ANSWERS)

1. Debit side
   Asset side
   Left side

2. Accounts receivable
   Accounts payable

3. Notes receivable

4. Cost of goods sold

5. A liability
   Accounts payable

6. Assets

7. Interest has been paid by the company
   Interest paid
   Prepaid interest

8. Reserve for depreciation
   Bad accounts shrinkage
   Depreciation
   Reserves

9. Sinking fund

10. General ledger (ledger)

———

TEST 2

DIRECTIONS: Directly and concisely, using brief answer form, answer the following questions.

1.   On what kind of account do payments on charge sales decrease the assets?

2.   In which ledger are customers accounts kept?

3.   What is the excess of resources over liabilities in closing the proprietor's account called?

4.   What are the calculations called that are necessary to prove the accuracy of the ledger records with a bank's statement of your checking account?

5.   In which book are records of materials bought by the firm entered?

6.   What is the book of original entry called?

7.   How should a transaction be posted when the firm sells merchandise to Mr. A. and charges this merchandise to his account?

8.   What does 2/10 (two, ten) mean on a bill or invoice?

9.   How do land and building accounts appear in the balance sheet?

10.   What is the inventory called that shows the material on hand at all times?

———

KEY (CORRECT ANSWERS)

1. Accounts receivable

2. Accounts receivable

3. Net capital
   Net worth
   Proprietorship

4. Reconciliation of bank account
   Bank reconcilement
   Reconciliation

5. Purchase ledger
   Purchase book
   Journal
   Record

6. Journal
   General journal

7. Debit (charge) Mr. A. or accounts receivable, and credit merchandise (sales)

8. 2% discount if paid within 10 days (2%, 10 days)

9. Fixed assets
   Assets

10. Perpetual inventory
    Running inventory

———

TEST 3

DIRECTIONS: Directly and concisely, using brief answer form, answer the following questions.

1. If an asset account is debited, what effect has this on the account?

2. What is the ledger to which the totals of the accounts in the daily ledger are transfered each month?

3. What account is debited when cash is withdrawn by the proprietor of a business for her personal use?

4. If a liability account is credited, what effect has this on the account?

5. What is the term for property or accounts receivable that are readily convertible into cash?

6. What are liabilities plus net worth equal to?

7. What is the result when cost of goods sold is deducted from the net sales?

8. What is a claim against a debtor listed as in the balance sheet?

———

KEY (CORRECT ANSWERS)

1. Increases it

2. General ledger

3. Proprietor's drawing account
    Personal account

4. Increases it

5. Liquid assets
    Current assets

6. Assets

7. Gross profits (sales)
    Margin

8. Assets
    Accounts receivable

———

ARITHMETICAL REASONING
EXAMINATION SECTION
TEST 1

DIRECTIONS: Each question or incomplete statement is followed by several suggested answers or completions. Select the one that BEST answers the question or completes the statement. *PRINT THE LETTER OF THE CORRECT ANSWER IN THE SPACE AT THE RIGHT.*

1. The initial mark-up in a store is 40%; mark-downs are 5%; shortages 1%; cash discounts 5%; alteration costs 5%; expenses 25%.
The maintained mark-up is

   A. 34%   B. 39%   C. 36.4%   D. 30%

   1.____

2. A buyer of TV sets wishes to maintain a mark-up of 37 1/2% after all mark-downs are taken. Of 25 sets costing $150 each, he sells 20 at $265.
How much can he mark-down the remaining 5 sets and still realize his mark-up objective?

   A. $166   B. $150   C. $140   D. $125

   2.____

3. An article originally selling for $12 and costing $8 was marked down to $10. Assuming the same markup,
what is the present market value of its cost?

   A. $6.68   B. $8.00   C. $5.67   D. $6.86

   3.____

4. What is the *on* percentage of trade discounts of 20% and 10%?

   A. 70   B. 85   C. 72   D. 80

   4.____

5. Canadian cost of a sweater is $40. Packing and labor cost $5.00; ad valorem duty, 40%; specific duty, 65¢; rate of exchange, .9091.
What is the duty in American currency?

   A. $16.96   B. $16.36   C. $18.00   D. $18.60

   5.____

6. A bolt of cloth measures 40 yards. The following yardages are sold: 4 1/2, 5 3/4, 6 7/8.
How many yards are left?

   A. 23 7/8   B. 22 1/2   C. 22 7/8   D. 24 3/8

   6.____

7. A shirt manufacturer has 76 1/2 yards of broadcloth to be used for shirts.
If each shirt takes 2 1/2 yards, how many shirts can he make?

   A. 38   B. 30   C. 19   D. 31

   7.____

8. Subtract 1.003 from 24.5.

   A. 24.003   B. 12.42   C. 23.2   D. 23.497

   8.____

9. A store carries a stock amounting to $265,830.25. Cash discounts, on the average, amount to 5 1/4%.
    How much are the cash discounts?

    A. $13,956.09   B. $1,395.61
    C. $139.56   D. $1.39

    9._____

10. If the sales in a department totaled $67,507.50 and the average sale was $22.50, how many transactions were there?

    A. 3,000   B. 300   C. 30,000   D. 30

    10._____

11. A department store reports a decrease in sales of 5.5% for this year.
    If this year's sales are $275,825,000, last year's sales were

    A. $291,878,000   B. $290,995,000
    C. $260,655,000   D. $290,788,000

    11._____

12. For the current year, the sales volume in a store was $50,000,000. Other income amounted to $1,500,000, Operating expenses were $10,000,000; cost of goods sold, $37,500,000.
    What is the percent of net profit based on retail?

    A. 10   B. 8   C. 50   D. 13

    12._____

13. If this year's sales show an increase of 300% over last year, this year's sales are how many times last year's sales?

    A. 3   B. 1 1/3   C. 4   D. 1/4

    13._____

14. Net sales in a shop amounted to $374,000; returns were 10%; allowances, 5%.
    What were the gross sales?

    A. $430,100   B. $415,000   C. $411,400   D. $440,000

    14._____

15. If the average sale in a store is expected to rise 5% over last year, and the number of transactions increases 3%, what percentage of increase in dollar sales volume should be planned?

    A. 8   B. 4   C. 8.15   D. 8.51

    15._____

16. The billed cost on an invoice is $300; freight charges, $10; cash discount, 2%; the retail value of the merchandise is $525.
    The mark-up percent on retail is

    A. 40.9   B. 42   C. 69   D. 69.5

    16._____

17. A hat costing $30.00 is to be given a mark-up of 45% on retail.
    The retail should be

    A. $43.50   B. $46.40   C. $55.40   D. $54.50

    17._____

18. Retail price $40 per unit; mark-up 40% of retail; transportation charge $1 per unit.
    Find billed cost that store can pay.

    A. $23   B. $24   C. $23.75   D. $24.75

    18._____

19. A buyer plans to spend $17,000 at retail for merchandise at a mark-up of 34%. He finds a special value at $3,000 that he can sell for $6,000.
What mark-up percentage does he need on the balance of his purchases in order to achieve his planned 34%?

    A. 35   B. 19.9   C. 15   D. 22.5

19.____

20. A store has a gross margin of 40% and reductions of 13%. Cash discount on purchases are not credited to the department. There are no alteration costs.
What is the initial mark-up?

    A. 46%   B. 53%   C. 27%   D. 26%

20.____

21. A dress is to retail for $35 with a mark-up of 40% of retail.
The cost of the dress to the retailer was

    A. $25   B. $21   C. $14   D. $20

21.____

22. The cost is $1.20 and the desired gross profit is 40% of retail.
The retail price should be

    A. $1.60   B. $1.68   C. $2.00   D. $2.40

22.____

23. The realized mark-up on a TV set is $50. The mark-up is 25% of retail.
The cost of the TV set to the retailer was

    A. $200   B. $125   C. $100   D. $150

23.____

24. Farnum, a salesman, earns $9.60 per hour for 40 hours a week, with time and a half for all hours over 40 per week. Last week, his total earnings were $470.40.
How many hours did he work last week?

    A. 46   B. 49   C. 47   D. 48

24.____

25. Dane & Clarke, partners, share profits in a 5:3 ratio. Dane's share of the profit for this year was $12,000 more than Clarke's share.
Clarke's share of the net profit was

    A. $30,000   B. $48,000   C. $36,000   D. $18,000

25.____

KEY (CORRECT ANSWERS)

1.	C	11.	A
2.	D	12.	B
3.	A	13.	C
4.	C	14.	D
5.	A	15.	C
6.	C	16.	A
7.	B	17.	D
8.	D	18.	A
9.	A	19.	B
10.	A	20.	A

21.	B
22.	C
23.	D
24.	A
25.	D

SOLUTIONS TO PROBLEMS

1. 5 + 5 − 1 = 9%. Then, (40%)(.91) = 36.4%.

2. (25)($150) = $3750 and $3750 .625 = $6000 total selling price of all sets. $6000 - (20)($265) = $700; 700 5 = $140 selling price for each of the last 5 sets. Markdown amount = $265 -$140 = $125

3. When the article's original selling price was $12, its cost was $8.00. If the article's original selling price were to be $10, it would cost $(8.00/12.00 x 10.00) = $6.67

4. Resulting percentage = (1-.20)(1-.10) = .72 = 72%

5. ($45)(.40) = $18, 18 + .65 = $18.65. Then, ($18.65)(.9091) = $16.95, closest to $16.96 in American currency.

6. 40 - 4 1/2 - 5 3/4 - 6 7/8 = 22 7/8 yds.

7. 76 1/2 ÷ 2 1/2 = 30.6, rounded down to 30 shirts

8. 24.5 - 1.003 = 23.497

9. ($265,830.25)(.0525) = $13,956.09

10. $67,507.50 $22.50 = 3000 transactions

11. $275,825,000 .945 = $291,878,000

12. $50,000,000 + $1,500,000 - $10,000,000 - $37,500,000 = $4,000,000 Then, $4,000,000 $50,000,000 = .08 = 8%

13. An increase of 300% over x = 4x, so sales are 4 times as large.

14. Gross sales = $374,000 .85 = $440,000

15. (1.05)(1.03) = 1.0815, which represents an 8.15% increase in dollar sales volume

16. $525 - $310 = $215; then, $215/$525 = 40.9%

17. $30 will represent 55% of retail amount. Thus, retail will be $30 .55 = $54.50

18. ($40)(.60) - $1 = $23

19. ($17,000)(1.34) = $22,780. Then, $22,780 - $6000 = $16,780. Also, $17,000 - $3,000 = $14,000. Finally, ($16,780 - $14,000) ÷ $14,000 ≈ 19.9%

20. Let x = markup percent. Then, x-40/x = .13 Solving, x = 46

21. Cost = ($35)(.60) = $21

22. Let x = retail price. Then, $1.20 = .60x. Solving, x = $2.00

23. $50 = 25% of retail, so retail = $200. Thus, cost = $200 - $50 = $150

24. Let x = overtime hours. Then, ($9.60)(40) + $14.40x = $470.40 Solving, x = 6. Total hours worked = 46

25. 5x - 3x - $12,000. So, x = $6000. Clarke's share = (3)($6000) = $18,000

———————

TEST 2

DIRECTIONS: Each question or incomplete statement is followed by several suggested answers or completions. Select the one that BEST answers the question or completes the statement. *PRINT THE LETTER OF THE CORRECT ANSWER IN THE SPACE AT THE RIGHT.*

1. Assume that you require 77 dozen felt practice golf balls. Which of the following represents the LOWEST bid for these balls?   1._____

    A.   41¢ per half-dozen less a *3%* discount
    B.   83¢ per dozen less a 7 1/2% discount
    C.   85¢ per dozen less a 10% discount
    D. $65.00 less a series discount of 3%, 2%

2. Assume that you require 1,944 rulers, packed 12 to the box, 18 boxes to the carton. Which of the following represents the LOWEST bid for these rulers?   2._____

    A.   5 1/2¢ per ruler
    B.   6¢ for the first 750 rulers; 5 1/2¢ for the next 750 rulers; 4 1/2¢ for every ruler thereafter
    C. $11.85 per carton
    D. $110 less series discounts of 2%, 1%

3. Assume that you require 20 cartons of colored raffia, cellophane wrapped in one lb. packages, 50 packages to the carton.
    Which of the following represents the LOWEST bid for the raffia?   3._____

    A.   8¢ per lb.; 15¢ per carton packing charge; 20¢ per carton delivery charge
    B.   9¢ per lb. less a 3% discount
    C.   10¢ per lb. for the first 150 lbs.; 9¢ per lb. for the next 200 lbs.; 80 for each lb. thereafter
    D. $83.50 less a 4 1/2% discount

4. Assume that you require 50 yards of table felt, 48" wide, and 12 yards of table felt, 72" wide.
    Which of the following represents the LOWEST bid for this felt?   4._____

    A.   32¢ per yard (48" wide), 40¢ per yard (72" wide)
    B.   34¢ per yard (48" wide), 43¢ per yard (72" wide); series discounts of 5%, 3%
    C.   360 per yard (48" wide), 41¢ per yard (72" wide); 8% discount, packing charge 75¢
    D. $23.00 for the order, 9% discount, packing charge 50¢

5. If the cost of 3 erasers is 5¢, the cost of 2 1/2 dozen erasers is   5._____

    A.   18¢   B.   37 1/2¢   C.   50¢   D.   31 1/2¢

6. A circle graph of a budget shows the expenditure of 26.2% for housing, 28.4% for food, 12% for clothing, 12.7% for taxes, and the balance for miscellaneous items. The percent for miscellaneous items is   6._____

    A.   31.5   B.   79.3   C.   20.7   D.   68.5

7. The cost of a broadloom rug measuring 4 feet by 6 feet, at $6.30 per square yard, is   7.____

     A. $16.80   B. $50.40   C. $37.60   D. $21.00

8. The number of tiles each measuring 2 inches by 3 inches needed for a wall 3 feet high   8.____
and 5 feet long is

     A.   180   B.   30   C.   360   D.   60

9. Assume that you require 4 tons of fertilizer. The fertilizer is packed in 100 pound bags.   9.____
Which of the following represents the LOWEST bid for the fertilizer?

     A.   6¢ per pound
     B. $5.50 per bag
     C. $7.00 for each of the first 30 bags; $5.00 for each bag thereafter
     D. $500.00 less 3 1/2% discount

10. Assume pencils are packed 5 gross to the case. A buyer requires 3,800 pencils each for   10.____
three departments and 2,700 pencils for another department. Assume that the vendor
will ship unbroken cases only directly to each department.
How many cases should he buy?

     A.   21   B.   22   C.   48   D.   49

11. Assume that a buyer had to purchase 40,000 lbs. of salt. Which one of the following bids   11.____
should he accept, assuming quality, service, and delivery terms are all the same?

     A.   1¢ per pound, 2%-30 days
     B.   99¢ per 100 lbs., 1%-30 days
     C. $19 per ton, 1%-30 days
     D. $18 per ton, net-30 days

12. Which one of the following four bids represents the BEST value, assuming delivery costs   12.____
amount to $100?

     A. $1,000 f.o.b. buyer, less 2%-10 days
     B. $900 f.o.b. seller, less 2%-10 days
     C. $975 delivered, net cash 30 days
     D. $990 f.o.b. buyer, less 1%-10 days

13. Suppose that four suppliers make the following offers to sell 2,000 units of a particular   13.____
commodity.
Which one is the MOST advan12tageous proposal?

     A. $10 list, less 40% and 5%
     B. $5 cost, plus 20% to cover overhead and profit
     C. $10 list, less 20% and 20%
     D. $5 cost, plus 10% overhead and 10% for profit

14. Suppose that you purchase 100 units of an item at a list of $1 per unit less 40% and   14.____
10%, and less 2% if paid within 10 days.
If payment is made within the 10-day limit, the amount of the payment should be

     A. $52.92   B. $54.00   C. $58.80   D. $60.00

15. Assume that the 1987 cost of living factor was 100 and that a certain product was selling   15.____
that year for $5 per unit. Assume further that at the present time the cost of living factor is
150.
If the selling price of the product increased 10% more than the cost of living during this
period, at the present time the product would be selling for ____ per unit.

   A. $8.25   B. $10.50   C. $16.50   D. $7.75

16. A certain food is sold in 4 ounce cans at 10 for $1.00 and in 1 pound cans at 3 for $1.00.   16.____
The savings in price per ounce by purchasing the food in the larger can is ____ cents/
ounce.

   A. .53   B. .35   C. .42   D. .68

17. After an article is discounted at 25%, it sells for $375. The ORIGINAL price of the article   17.____
was

   A. $93.75   B. $350   C. $375   D. $500

18. Assume that you require 1,440 pencils, packed 12 to the box, 24 boxes to the carton.   18.____
Which of the following represents the LOWEST bid for these pencils?

   A. 2¢ per pencil
   B. $6.50 per carton
   C. 27¢ per box less a 4% discount
   D. $40 less a 3% discount

19. If erasers cost 8¢ each for the first 250, 70 each for the next 250, and 5¢ for every eraser   19.____
thereafter, how many erasers may be purchased for $50?

   A. 600   B. 750   C. 850   D. 1,000

20. Assume that a buyer saves $14 on the purchase of an item that is discounted at 25%.   20.____
The amount of money that the buyer must pay for the item is

   A. $42   B. $52   C. $54   D. $56

Questions 21-24.

DIRECTIONS: Questions 21 through 24 are to be answered on the basis of the following
method of obtaining a reorder point: multiply the monthly rate of consumption
by the lead time (in months) and add the minimum balance.

21. If the lead time is one-half month, the minimum balance is 6 units, and the monthly rate   21.____
of consumption is 4 units, then the reorder point is ___ units.

   A. 4   B. 6   C. 8   D. 12

22. If the reorder point is 25 units, the lead time is 3 months, and the minimum balance is 10   22.____
units, then the average monthly rate of consumption is ____ units.

   A. 3   B. 5   C. 6   D. 10

23. If the reorder point is 400 units, the lead time is 2 months, and the monthly rate of con-   23.____
sumption is 150 units, then the minimum balance is _____units.

   A. 50   B. 100   C. 150   D. 200

24. If the reorder point is 75 units, the monthly rate of consumption is 60 units, and the minimum balance is 45 units, then the lead time is _____month(s).

    A. 1/2   B. 1   C. 2   D. 4

24.____

25. A purchasing office has 4,992 special requisitions to be processed. Working alone,
Buyer A could process these in 30 days; working alone, Buyer B could process these in
40 days; working alone, Buyer C could process these in 60 days.
The LEAST number of days in which Buyers A, B, and C working together can process
these 4,992 special requisitions is APPROXIMATELY_____ days.

    A. 14   B. 20   C. 34   D. 45

25.____

KEY (CORRECT ANSWERS)

1.	C		11.	D
2.	B		12.	C
3.	D		13.	A
4.	B		14.	A
5.	C		15.	A
6.	C		16.	C
7.	A		17.	D
8.	C		18.	A
9.	B		19.	B
10.	B		20.	A

21.	C
22.	B
23.	B
24.	A
25.	A

SOLUTIONS TO PROBLEMS

1. Bid A = (.82)(77)(.97) $\approx$ \$61.25;
    Bid B = (.83)(77)(.925) $\approx$ \$59.12
    Bid C = (.85)(77)(.90) $\approx$ \$58.91;
    Bid D = (\$65.00)(.97)(.98) $\approx$ \$61.79 Thus, Bid C is lowest.

2. Bid A = (.055)(1944) = \$106.92;
    Bid B = (.06)(750)+(.055)(750) + (.045)(444) = \$106.23;
    Bid C = (\$11.85)(9) = \$106.65;
    Bid D = (\$110)(.98)(.99) $\approx$ \$106.72. Thus, Bid B is lowest.

3. Bid A = (.08)(1000) + (.15)(20) + (.20)(20) = \$87.00
    Bid B = (.09)(1000)(.97) = \$87.30
    Bid C = (.10)(150) + (.09)(200) + (.08)(650) = \$85.00
    Bid D = (\$83.50)(.955) $\approx$ \$79.74
    Thus, Bid D is lowest.

4. Bid A = (.32)(50)+(.40)(12) = \$20.80
    Bid B = (.34)(50)+(.43)(12) = \$22.16; so (\$22.16)(.95)(.97) $\approx$ \$20.42
    Bid C = (.36)(50)+(.41)(12) = \$22.92; so (\$22.92)(.92)+.75 $\approx$ \$21.84
    Bid D = (\$23.00)(.91)+.50 = \$21.43
    Bid B is lowest.

5. (2 1/2)(12) = 30 erasers, which will cost (.05)(10) = 50¢

6. 100 - 26.2 - 28.4 - 12 - 12.7 = 20.7% for miscellaneous items

7. 24 $\div$ 9 = 2 2/3 sq.yds. Then, (\$6.30)(2 2/3) = \$16.80

8. 3' 2" = 18; 5' 3" = 20. Thus, (18)(20) = 360 tiles

9. Bid A = (.06)(8000) = \$480
    Bid B = (\$5.50)(80) = \$440
    Bid C = (\$7.00)(30)+(\$5.00)(50) = \$460 Bid D - (\$500)(.965) = \$482.50 Thus,
    Bid B is lowest.

10. 5 gross = 5(144) = 720; 3800 will be 6 unbroken cases x 3 = 18
    2700 will be 4 unbroken cases = 4
    ―――
    22

11. Bid A = (.01)(40,000)(.98) = \$392.00
    Bid B = (.99)(400)(.99) = \$392.04
    Bid C = (\$19)(20)(.99) = \$376.20
    Bid D = (\$18)(20) = \$360.00
    Bid D is lowest.

12. A. 1,000 - 2% = 980
    B. 900 + 100 - 2% = 980

C. 975
D. 990 - 9.90 = 980.10
C is best value

13. Proposal A: ($10)(.60)(.95) = $5.70
Proposal B: $5 + ($5)(.20) = $6.00
Proposal C: ($10) (.80)(.80) = $6.40
Proposal D: $5 + (.20)($5) = $6.00
Proposal A is lowest.

14. Payment = ($100)(.60)(.90)(.98) = $52.92

15. Present cost = ($5)(1.50)(1.10) = $8.25

16. 40 ounces for $1.00 in smaller cans means 2.5 cents per ounce. For the larger cans, (3)(16) = 48 ounces for $1.00, which means 2.08$\overline{3}$ cents per ounce. The savings is approximately .42 cents per ounce.

17. Original price = $375 ÷ .75 = $500

18. Bid A = (1440)(.02) = $28.80
Bid B = (1440 ÷ 288)($6.50) = $32.50
Bid C = [(144 ÷ 12)(.27)] [.96] = $31.10
Bid D = ($40)(.97) = $38.80
Bid A is lowest.

19. 250 erasers cost (250)(.08) = $20
500 erasers cost $20 + (250)(.07) = $37.50
The number of additional erasers = ($50 - $37.50) ÷ .05 = 250
Total number of erasers = 750

20. $14 ÷ .25 = $56. Then, $56 - $14 = $42

21. (4)(.5) +6 = 8 units

22. Let x = monthly rate. Then, (x)(3) + 10 = 25. Solving, x = 5 units

23. Let x = minimum balance. (150)(2) + x = 400. Solving, x = 100 units

24. Let x = lead time. (60)(x) + 45 = 75. Solving, x = 1/2 month

25. Buyer A does 4992 ÷ 30 ≈ 166 per day
Buyer B does 4992 ÷ 40 ≈ 125 per day
Buyer C does 4992 ÷ 60 ≈ 83 per day
Working together, approximately 374 requisitions are done per day. Finally, 4992 ÷ 374 ≈ 13, closest to 14 in selections.

ARITHMETICAL REASONING
EXAMINATION SECTION
TEST 1

DIRECTIONS: Each question or incomplete statement is followed by
several suggested answers or completions. Select the
one that BEST answers the question or completes the
statement. *PRINT THE LETTER OF THE CORRECT ANSWER IN
THE SPACE AT THE RIGHT.*

1. The ABC Corporation had a gross income of $125,500.00 in   1.___
    2004. Of this, it paid 60% for overhead.
    If the gross income for 2005 increased by $6,500 and the
    cost of overhead increased to 61% of gross income, how
    much MORE did it pay for overhead in 2005 than in 2004?
        A. $1,320   B. $5,220   C. $7,530   D. $8,052

2. After one year, Mr. Richards paid back a total of $16,950   2.___
    as payment for a $15,000 loan. All the money paid over
    $15,000 was simple interest.
    The interest charge was MOST NEARLY
        A. 13%   B. 11%   C. 9%   D. 7%

3. A checking account has a balance of $253.36.   3.___
    If deposits of $36.95, $210.23, and $7.34 and withdrawals
    of $117.35, $23.37, and $15.98 are made, what is the NEW
    balance of the account?
        A. $155.54   B. $351.18   C. $364.58   D. $664.58

4. In 2004, The W Realty Company spent 27% of its income on   4.___
    rent.
    If it earned $97,254 in 2004, the amount it paid for rent
    was
        A. $26,258.58   B. $26,348.58
        C. $27,248.58   D. $27,358.58

5. Six percent simple annual interest on $2,436.18 is MOST   5.___
    NEARLY
        A. $145.08   B. $145.17   C. $146.08   D. $146.17

6. H. Partridge receives a weekly gross salary (before deduc-   6.___
    tions) of $397.50. Through weekly payroll deductions of
    $13.18, he is paying back a loan he took from his pension
    fund.
    If other fixed weekly deductions amount to $122.76, how
    much pay would Mr. Partridge take home over a period of
    33 weeks?
        A. $7,631.28   B. $8,250.46   C. $8,631.48   D. $13,117.50

7. Mr. Robertson is a city employee enrolled in a city   7.___
    retirement system. He has taken out a loan from the
    retirement fund and is paying it back at the rate of
    $14.90 every two weeks.
    In eighteen weeks, how much money will he have paid back
    on the loan?
        A. $268.20   B. $152.80   C. $134.10   D. $67.05

8. In 2004, The Iridor Book Company had the following
   expenses: rent, $6,500; overhead, $52,585; inventory,
   $35,700; and miscellaneous, $1,275.
   If all of these expenses went up 18% in 2005, what
   would they TOTAL in 2005?
   A. $17,290.80   B. $78,769.20
   C. $96,060.00   D. $113,350.80

9. Ms. Ranier had a gross salary of $710.72 paid once every
   two weeks.
   If the deductions from each paycheck are $125.44, $50.26,
   $12.58, and $2.54, how much money would Ms. Ranier take
   home in eight weeks?
   A. $2,079.60   B. $2,842.88   C. $4,159.20   D. $5,685.76

10. Mr. Martin had a net income of $95,500 in 2004.
    If he spent 34% on rent and household expenses, 3% on
    house furnishings, 25% on clothes, and 36% on food, how
    much was left for savings and other expenses?
    A. $980   B. $1,910   C. $3,247   D. $9,800

11. Mr. Elsberg can pay back a loan of $1,800 from the city
    employees' retirement system if he pays back $36.69
    every two weeks for two full years.
    At the end of the two years, how much more than the
    original $1,800 he borrowed will Mr. Elsberg have paid
    back?
    A. $53.94   B. $107.88   C. $190.79   D. $214.76

12. Mr. Nusbaum is a city employee receiving a gross salary
    (salary before deductions) of $20,800. Every two weeks
    the following deductions are taken out of his salary:
    Federal Income Tax, $162.84; FICA, $44.26; State Tax,
    $29.72; City Tax, $13.94; Health Insurance, $3.14.
    If Mr. Nusbaum's salary and deductions remained the same
    for a full calendar year, what would his net salary
    (gross salary less deductions) be in that year?
    A. $6,596.20   B. $14,198.60
    C. $18,745.50   D. $20,546.30

13. Add: 8936
           7821
           8953
           4297
           9785
           6579

    A. 45,371   B. 45,381   C. 46,371   D. 46,381

14. Multiply: 987
                867

    A. 854,609   B. 854,729   C. 855,709   D. 855,729

15. Divide: 59)$\overline{321439.0}$ 15.___

     A. 5438.1   B. 5447.1   C. 5448.1   D. 5457.1

16. Divide: .057)$\overline{721}$ 16.___

     A. 12,648.0   B. 12,648.1   C. 12,649.0   D. 12,649.1

17. If the total number of employees in one city agency   17.___
increased from 1,927 to 2,006 during a certain year,
the percentage increase in the number of employees for
that year is MOST NEARLY
     A. 4%   B. 5%   C. 6%   D. 7%

18. During a single fiscal year, which totaled 248 workdays,   18.___
one account clerk verified 1,488 purchase vouchers.
Assuming a normal work week of five days, what is the
AVERAGE number of vouchers verified by the account clerk
in a one-week period during this fiscal year?
     A. 25   B. 30   C. 35   D. 40

19. Multiplying a number by .75 is the same as   19.___
     A. multiplying it by 2/3   B. dividing it by 2/3
     C. multiplying it by 3/4   D. dividing it by 3/4

20. In City Agency A, 2/3 of the employees are enrolled in   20.___
a retirement system. City Agency B has the same number
of employees as Agency A, and 60% of these are enrolled
in a retirement system.
If Agency A has a total of 660 employees, how many MORE
employees does it have enrolled in a retirement system
than does Agency B?
     A. 36   B. 44   C. 56   D. 66

21. Net worth is equal to assets minus liabilities.   21.___
If, at the end of 2003, a textile company had assets of
$98,695.83 and liabilities of $59,238.29, what was its
net worth?
     A. $38,478.54   B. $38,488.64
     C. $39,457.54   D. $48,557.54

22. Mr. Martin's assets consist of the following: 22.___
         Cash on hand $ 5,233.74
         Automobile   3,206.09
         Furniture   4,925.00
         Government Bonds   5,500.00
         House   36,690.85
What are his TOTAL assets?
     A. $54,545.68   B. $54,455.68
     C. $55,455.68   D. $55,555.68

23. If Mr. Mitchell has $627.04 in his checking account and
    then writes three checks for $241.75, $13.24, and $102.97,
    what will be his new balance?
    A. $257.88   B. $269.08   C. $357.96   D. $369.96

23.___

24. An employee's net pay is equal to his total earnings less
    all deductions.
    If an employee's total earnings in a pay period are
    $497.05, what is his net pay if he has the following
    deductions: Federal income tax, $90.32; FICA, $28.74;
    State tax, $18.79; City tax, $7.25; Pension, $1.88?
    A. $351.17   B. $351.07   C. $350.17   D. $350.07

24.___

25. A petty cash fund had an opening balance of $85.75 on
    December 1. Expenditures of $23.00, $15.65, $5.23,
    $14.75, and $26.38 were made out of this fund during
    the first 14 days of the month. Then, on December 17,
    another $38.50 was added to the fund.
    If additional expenditures of $17.18, $3.29, and $11.64
    were made during the remainder of the month, what was
    the FINAL balance of the petty cash fund at the end of
    December?
    A. $6.93   B. $7.13   C. $46.51   D. $91.40

25.___

KEY (CORRECT ANSWERS)

1. B		11. B	
2. A		12. B	
3. B		13. C	
4. A		14. D	
5. D		15. C	
6. C		16. D	
7. C		17. A	
8. D		18. B	
9. A		19. C	
10. B		20. B	

21. C
22. D
23. B
24. D
25. B

SOLUTIONS TO PROBLEMS

1. ($132,000)(.61)-($125,500)(.60) = $5220

2. Interest = $1950. As a percent, $1950 ÷ 15,000 = 13%

3. New balance = $253.36 + $36.95 + $210.23 + $7.34 - $117.35 - $23.37 - $15.98 = $351.18

4. Rent = ($97,254)(.27) = $26,258.58

5. ($2436.18)(.06) ≈ $146.17

6. ($397.50-$13.18-$122.76)(33) = $8631.48

7. ($14.90)($\frac{18}{2}$) = $134.10

8. ($6500+$52,585+$35,700+$1275)(1.18) = $113,350.80

9. ($710.72-$125.44-$50.26-$12.58-$2.54)($\frac{8}{2}$) = $2079.60

10. (1-.34-.03-.25-.36)($95,500) = $1910

11. ($36.69)(52) - $1800 = $107.88

12. $20,800 - (26)($162.84+$44.26+$29.72+$13.94+$3.14) = $14,198.60

13. 8936 + 7821 + 8953 + 4297 + 9785 + 6579 = 46,371

14. (987)(867) = 855,729

15. 321,439 ÷ 59 ≈ 5448.1

16. 721 ÷ .057 ≈ 12,649.1

17. (2006-1927) ÷ 1927 ≈ 4%

18. Let x = number of vouchers. Then, $\frac{x}{5} = \frac{1488}{248}$. Solving, x = 30

19. Multiplying by .75 is equivalent to multiplying by $\frac{3}{4}$

20. (660)($\frac{2}{3}$) - (660)(.60) = 44

21. Net worth = $98,695.83 - $59,238.29 = $39,457.54

22. Total assets = $5233.74 + $3206.09 + $4925.00 + $5500.00 + $36,690.85 = $55,555.68

23. New balance = $627.04 - $241.75 - $13.24 - $102.97 = $269.08

24. Net pay = $497.05 - $90.32 - $28.74 - $18.79 - $7.25 - $1.88 = $350.07

25. Final balance = $85.75 - $23.00 - $15.65 - $5.23 - $14.75 - $26.38 + $38.50 - $17.18 - $3.29 - $11.64 = $7.13

TEST 2

DIRECTIONS: Each question or incomplete statement is followed by several suggested answers or completions. Select the one that BEST answers the question or completes the statement. *PRINT THE LETTER OF THE CORRECT ANSWER IN THE SPACE AT THE RIGHT.*

1. The formula for computing base salary is: Earnings equals base gross plus additional gross.
   If an employee's earnings during a particular period are in the amounts of $597.45, $535.92, $639.91, and $552.83, and his base gross salary is $525.50 per paycheck, what is the TOTAL of the additional gross earned by the employee during that period?
   A. $224.11   B. $224.21   C. $224.51   D. $244.11

   1.___

2. If a lump sum death benefit is paid by the retirement system in an amount equal to 3/7 of an employee's last yearly salary of $13,486.50, the amount of the death benefit paid is MOST NEARLY
   A. $5,749.29   B. $5,759.92   C. $5,779.92   D. $5,977.29

   2.___

3. Suppose that a member has paid 15 installments on a 28-installment loan.
   The percentage of the number of installments paid to the retirement system is
   A. 53.57%   B. 53.97%   C. 54.57%   D. 55.37%

   3.___

4. If an employee takes a 1-month vacation during a calendar year, the percentage of the year during which he works is MOST NEARLY
   A. 90.9%   B. 91.3%   C. 91.6%   D. 92.1%

   4.___

5. Suppose that an employee took a leave of absence totaling 7 months during a calendar year.
   Assuming the employee did not take any vacation time during the remainder of that year, the percentage of the year in which he worked is MOST NEARLY
   A. 41.7%   B. 43.3%   C. 46.5%   D. 47.1%

   5.___

6. A member has borrowed $4,725 from her funds in the retirement system.
   If $3,213 has been repaid, the percentage of the loan which is still outstanding is MOST NEARLY
   A. 16%   B. 32%   C. 48%   D. 68%

   6.___

7. If an employee worked only 24 weeks during the year because of illness, the portion of the year he was out of work was MOST NEARLY
   A. 46%   B. 48%   C. 51%   D. 54%

   7.___

8. If an employee purchased credit for a 16-week period of
   service which he had prior to rejoining the retirement
   system, the percentage of a year he purchased credit
   for was MOST NEARLY
      A. 27.9%   B. 28.8%   C. 30.7%   D. 33.3%
           8.___

9. If an employee contributes 2/11 of his yearly salary to
   his pension fund account, the percentage of his yearly
   salary which he contributes is MOST NEARLY
      A. 17.9%   B. 18.2%   C. 18.4%   D. 19.0%
           9.___

10. In 1975, the maximum amount of income from which social
    security tax could be withheld (base salary) was $14,100.
    In 1977, the base salary was $16,500.
    The 1977 base salary represents a percentage increase
    over the 1975 base salary of approximately
       A. 15%   B. 16%   C. 17%   D. 18%
            10.___

11. If 17.5% of an employee's salary is withheld for taxes,
    the one of the following which is the fraction of the
    salary withheld is
       A. 3/20   B. 8/35   C. 7/40   D. 4/25
            11.___

12. If a person withdraws 42% of the funds from his account
    with the retirement system, the remaining balance repre-
    sents a fraction of MOST NEARLY
       A. 7/13   B. 5/9   C. 7/12   D. 4/7
            12.___

13. A property decreases in value from $45,000 to $35,000.
    The percent of decrease is MOST NEARLY
       A. 20.5%   B. 22.2%   C. 25.0%   D. 28.6%
            13.___

14. The fraction $\frac{487}{101326}$ expressed as a decimal is MOST NEARLY
       A. .0482   B. .00481   C. .0049   D. .00392
            14.___

15. The reciprocal of the sum of 2/3 and 1/6 can be expressed
    as
       A. 0.83   B. 1.20   C. 1.25   D. 1.50
            15.___

16. Total land and building costs for a new commercial proper-
    ty equal $50 per square foot.
    If the investors expect a 10 percent return on their
    costs, and if total operating expenses average 5 percent
    of total costs, annual gross rentals per square foot must
    be AT LEAST
       A. $7.50   B. $8.50   C. $10.00   D. $12.00
            16.___

17. The formula for computing the amount of annual deposit in
    a compound interest bearing account to provide a lump sum
    at the end of a period of years is $X = \dfrac{r.L}{(1+r)^{n}-1}$ (X is the
    amount of annual deposit, r is the rate of interest, and
    n is the number of years) and L = lump sum)
            17.___

Using the formula, the annual amount of the deposit at
the end of each year to accumulate to $20,000 at the end
of 3 years with interest at 2 percent on annual balances
is
    A. $6,120.00 B. $6,203.33 C. $6,535.09 D. $6,666.66

18. An investor sold two properties at $150,000 each. On one   18.___
he made a 25 percent profit. On the other he suffered a
25 percent loss.
The NET result of his sales was
    A. neither a gain nor a loss
    B. a $20,000 loss
    C. a $75,000 gain
    D. a $75,000 loss

19. A contractor decides to install a chain fence covering   19.___
the perimeter of a parcel 75 feet wide and 112 feet in
depth.
Which one of the following represents the number of feet
to be covered?
    A. 187   B. 364   C. 374   D. 8,400

20. A builder estimates he can build an average of $4\frac{1}{2}$ one-   20.___
family homes to an acre. There are 640 acres to one
square mile.
Which one of the following CORRECTLY represents the
number of one-family homes the builder would estimate he
can build on one square mile?
    A. 1,280   B. 1,920   C. 2,560   D. 2,880

21. $.01059 deposited at 7 percent interest will yield $1.00   21.___
in 30 years.
If a person deposited $1,059 at 7 percent interest on
April 1, 1974, which one of the following amounts would
represent the worth of this deposit on March 31, 2004?
    A. $100   B. $1,000   C. $10,000   D. $100,000

22. A building has an economic life of forty years.   22.___
Assuming the building depreciates at a constant annual
rate, which one of the following CORRECTLY represents
the yearly percentage of depreciation?
    A. 2.0%   B. 2.5%   C. 5.0%   D. 7.0%

23. A building produces a gross income of $200,000 with a   23.___
net income of $20,000, before mortgage charges and capital
recapture. The owner is able to increase the gross
income 5 percent without a corresponding increase in
operating costs.
The effect upon the net income will be an INCREASE of
    A. 5%   B. 10%   C. 12.5%   D. 50%

24. The present value of $1.00 not payable for 8 years, and   24.___
    at 10 percent interest, is $.4665.
    Which of the following amounts represents the PRESENT
    value of $1,000 payable 8 years hence at 10 percent
    interest?
       A. $46.65   B. $466.50   C. $4,665.00 D. $46,650.00

25. The amount of real property taxes to be levied by a city   25.___
    is $100 million. The assessment roll subject to taxation
    shows an assessed valuation of $2 billion.
    Which one of the following tax rates CORRECTLY represents
    the tax rate to be levied per $100 of assessed valuation?
       A. $.50   B. $5.00   C. $50.00   D. $500.00

KEY (CORRECT ANSWERS)

1. A		11. C	
2. C		12. C	
3. A		13. B	
4. C		14. B	
5. A		15. B	
6. B		16. A	
7. D		17. C	
8. C		18. B	
9. B		19. C	
10. C		20. D	

21. D
22. B
23. D
24. B
25. B

SOLUTIONS TO PROBLEMS

1. $597.45 + $535.92 + $639.91 + $552.83 = $2326.11
   Then, $2326.11 - (4)($525.50) = $224.11

2. Death benefit = ($13,486.50)$(\frac{3}{7})$ ≈ $5779.92

3. $\frac{15}{28}$ ≈ 53.57%

4. $\frac{11}{12}$ ≈ 91.6% (closer to 91.7%)

5. $\frac{5}{12}$ ≈ 41.7%

6. ($4725-$3213) ÷ $4725 ≈ 32%

7. $\frac{28}{52}$ ≈ 54%

8. $\frac{16}{52}$ ≈ 30.7% (closer to 30.8%)

9. $\frac{2}{11}$ ≈ 18.2%

10. ($16,500-$14,100) ÷ $14,100 ≈ 17%

11. 17.5% = $\frac{175}{1000}$ = $\frac{7}{40}$

12. 100% - 42% = 58% = $\frac{58}{100}$ = $\frac{29}{50}$, closest to $\frac{7}{12}$ in selections

13. $\frac{\$10,000}{\$45,000}$ ≈ 22.2%

14. 487/101,326 ≈ .00481

15. $\frac{2}{3}$ + $\frac{1}{6}$ = $\frac{5}{6}$ Then, 1 ÷ $\frac{5}{6}$ = $\frac{6}{5}$ = 1.20

16. (.15)($50) = $7.50

17. x = (.02)($20,000)/[(1+.02)^3-1] = 400 ÷ .061208 ≈ $6535.09

18. Sold 150,000, 25% loss = paid 200,000, loss of 50,000
    Sold 150,000, 25% profit = paid 120,000, profit of 30,000
    - 50,000 + 30,000 = -20,000 (loss)

19. Perimeter = (2)(75')+(2)(112') = 374 ft.

20. (640)($4\frac{1}{2}$) = 2880 homes

21. $(1 \div .01059)(1059) = \$100,000$

22. $1 \div 40 = .025 = 2.5\%$

23. New gross income = $(\$200,000)(1.05) = \$210,000$.
    Then, $(\$210,000 - \$200,000) \div \$20,000 = 50\%$

24. Let x = present value of \$1000. Then, $\dfrac{\$1.00}{\$.4665} = \dfrac{\$1000}{x}$

    Solving, x = \$466.50

25. Let x = tax rate. Then, $\dfrac{\$100,000,000}{\$2,000,000,000} = \dfrac{x}{\$100}$

    Solving, x = \$5.00

TEST 3

DIRECTIONS: Each question or incomplete statement is followed by several suggested answers or completions. Select the one that BEST answers the question or completes the statement. *PRINT THE LETTER OF THE CORRECT ANSWER IN THE SPACE AT THE RIGHT.*

1. It is found that for the past three years the average weekly number of inspections per inspector ranged from 20 inspections to 40 inspections.
   On the basis of this information, it is MOST reasonable to conclude that
   A. on the average, 30 inspections per week were made
   B. the average weekly number of inspections never fell below 20
   C. the performance of inspectors deteriorated over the three-year period
   D. the range in average weekly inspections was 60

1.___

Questions 2-4.

DIRECTIONS: Questions 2 through 4 are to be answered on the basis of the following information.

The number of students admitted to University X in 2004 from High School Y was 268 students. This represented 13.7 percent of University X's entering freshman classes. In 2005, it is expected that University X will admit 591 students from High School Y, which is expected to represent 19.4 percent of the 2005 entering freshman classes of University X.

2. Which of the following is the CLOSEST estimate of the size of University X's expected 2005 entering freshman classes?
   ___ students.
   A. 2,000   B. 2,500   C. 3,000   D. 3,500

2.___

3. Of the following, the expected percentage of increase from 2004 to 2005 in the number of students graduating from High School Y and entering University X as freshmen is MOST NEARLY
   A. 5.7%   B. 20%   C. 45%   D. 120%

3.___

4. Assume that the cost of processing each freshman admission to University X from High School Y in 2004 was an average of $28. Also, that this was 1/3 more than the average cost of processing each of the other 2004 freshman admissions to University X.
   Then, the one of the following that MOST closely shows the total processing cost of all 2004 freshman admissions to University X is
   A. $6,500   B. $20,000   C. $30,000   D. $40,000

4.___

5. Assume that during the fiscal year 2005-2006, a bureau produced 20% more work units than it produced in the fiscal year 2004-2005. Also assume that during the fiscal year 2005-2006 that bureau's staff was 20% smaller than it was in the fiscal year 2004-2005.
On the basis of this information, it would be MOST proper to conclude that the number of work units produced per staff member in that bureau in the fiscal year 2005-2006 exceeded the number of work units produced per staff member in that bureau in the fiscal year 2004-2005 by which one of the following percentages?
A. 20%   B. 25%   C. 40%   D. 50%

6. Assume that during the following five fiscal years (FY), a bureau has received the following appropriations:
FY 2002-2003 - $200,000
FY 2003-2004 - $240,000
FY 2004-2005 - $280,000
FY 2005-2006 - $390,000
FY 2006-2007 - $505,000
The bureau's appropriation for which one of the following fiscal years showed the LARGEST percentage of increase over the bureau's appropriation for the immediately previous fiscal year?
A. FY 2003-2004   B. FY 2004-2005
C. FY 2005-2006   D. FY 2006-2007

7. Assume that the number of buses (U_t) required for a given line-haul system serving the Central Business District depends upon roundtrip time (t), capacity of bus (c), and the total number of people to be moved in a peak hour (P) in the major direction, i.e., in the morning and out in the evening.
The formula for the number of buses required is

A. $U_t = Ptc$ B. $U_t = \dfrac{tP}{c}$ C. $U_t = \dfrac{cP}{t}$ D. $U_t = \dfrac{ct}{P}$

8. The area, in blocks, that can be served by a single stop for any maximum walking distance is given by the following formula: $a = 2w^2$. In this formula, a = the area served by a stop, and w = maximum walking distance.
If people will tolerate a walk of up to three blocks, how many stops would be needed to service an area of 288 square blocks?
A. 9   B. 16   C. 18   D. 27

Questions 9-11.

DIRECTIONS: Questions 9 through 11 are to be answered on the basis of the following information.

In 2006, a police precinct records 456 cases of car thefts which is 22.6 percent of all grand larcenies. In 2007, there were 560 such cases, which constituted 35% of the broader category.

9. The number of crimes in the broader category in 2007 was   9.___
   MOST NEARLY
   A. 1,600   B. 1,700   C. 1,960   D. 2,800

10. The change from 2006 to 2007 in the number of crimes in   10.___
    the broader category represented MOST NEARLY a
    A. 2.5% decrease   B. 10.1% increase
    C. 12.5% increase   D. 20% decrease

11. In 2007, one out of every 6 of these crimes was solved.   11.___
    This represents MOST NEARLY what percentage of the total
    number of crimes in the broader category that year?
    A. 5.8   B. 6   C. 9.3   D. 12

12. Assume that a maintenance shop does 5 brake jobs to every   12.___
    3 front-end jobs. It does 8,000 jobs altogether in a
    240-day year. In one day, one worker can do 3 front-end
    jobs or 4 brake jobs.
    About how many workers will be needed in the shop?
    A. 3   B. 5   C. 10   D. 18

13. Assume that the price of a certain item declines by 6%   13.___
    one year, and then increases by 5 and 10 percent, respec-
    tively, during the next two years.
    What is the OVERALL increase in price over the three-year
    period?
    A. 4.2   B. 6   C. 8.6   D. 10.1

14. After finding the total percent change in a price (TC)   14.___
    over a three-year period, as in the preceding question,
    one could compute the average annual percent change in
    the price by using the formula

    A. $(1 + TC)^{1/3}$ B. $\dfrac{(1 + TC)}{3}$

    C. $(1 + TC)^{1/3} - 1$ D. $\dfrac{1}{(1 + TC)^{1/3} - 1}$

15. 357 is 6% of   15.___
    A. 2,142   B. 5,950   C. 4,140   D. 5,900

16. In 2002, a department bought n pieces of a certain supply   16.___
    item for a total of $x. In 2003, the department bought
    k percent fewer of the item but had to pay a total of g
    percent more for it.
    Which of the following formulas is CORRECT for determining
    the average price per item in 2003?
    A. $100 \dfrac{xg}{nk}$ B. $\dfrac{x(100 + g)}{n(100 - k)}$

    C. $\dfrac{x(100 - g)}{n(100 + k)}$ D. $\dfrac{x}{n} - 100 \dfrac{g}{k}$

17. A sample of 18 income tax returns, each with 4 personal exemptions, is taken for 2001 and for 2002. The break-down is as follows in terms of income:

Average gross income (in thousands)	Number of returns 2001	2002
40	6	2
80	10	11
120	2	5

There is a personal deduction per exemption of $500. There are no other expense deductions. In addition, there is an exclusion of $3,000 for incomes less than $50,000 and $2,000 for incomes from $50,000 to $99,999.99. From $100,000 upward there is no exclusion.
The average net taxable income for the samples in thousands) for 2001 is MOST NEARLY
   A. $67   B. $85   C. $10   D. $128   17.___

18. In the preceding question, the increase in average net taxable income for the sample (in thousands) between 2001 and 2002 is
   A. 16   B. 20   C. 24   D. 34   18.___

19. Assume that supervisor S has four subordinates - A, B, C, and D.
The MAXIMUM number of relationships, assuming that all combinations are included, that can exist between S and his subordinates is
   A. 28   B. 15   C. 7   D. 4   19.___

20. If the workmen's compensation insurance rate for clerical workers is 93 cents per $100 of wages, the total premium paid by a city whose clerical staff earns $8,765,000 is MOST NEARLY
   A. $8,150   B. $81,515   C. $87,650   D. $93,765   20.___

21. Assume that a budget of $3,240,000,000 for the fiscal year beginning July 1, 2003 has been approved. A city sales tax is expected to provide $1,100,000,000; licenses, fees and sundry revenues are expected to yield $121,600,000; the balance is to be raised from property taxes. A tax equalization board has appraised all property in the city at a fair value of $42,500,000,000. The council wishes to assess property at 60% of its fair value.
The tax rate would need to be MOST NEARLY _____ per $100 of assessed value.
   A. $12.70   B. $10.65   C. $7.90   D. $4.00   21.___

22. Men's white linen handkerchiefs cost $12.90 for 3.
The cost per dozen handkerchiefs is
   A. $77.40   B. $38.70   C. $144.80   D. $51.60   22.___

23. Assume that it is necessary to partition a room measuring 40 feet by 20 feet into eight smaller rooms of equal size. Allowing no room for aisles, the MINIMUM amount of partitioning that would be needed is _____ feet.
    A. 90   B. 100   C. 110   D. 140

23.___

24. Assume that two types of files have been ordered: 200 of type A and 100 of type B. When the files are delivered, the buyer discovers that 25% of each type is damaged. Of the remaining files, 20% of type A and 40% of type B are the wrong color.
    The total number of files that are the WRONG COLOR is
    A. 30   B. 40   C. 50   D. 60

24.___

25. In a unit of five inspectors, one inspector makes an average of 12 inspections a day, two inspectors make an average of 20 inspections a day, and two inspectors make an average of 9 inspections a day.
    If in a certain week one of the inspectors who makes an average of nine inspections a day is out of work on Monday and Tuesday because of illness and all the inspectors do no inspections for half a day on Wednesday because of a special meeting, the number of inspections this unit can be expected to make in that week is MOST NEARLY
    A. 215   B. 225   C. 230   D. 250

25.___

KEY (CORRECT ANSWERS)

1. B		11. A	
2. C		12. C	
3. D		13. C	
4. D		14. C	
5. D		15. B	
6. C		16. B	
7. B		17. A	
8. B		18. A	
9. A		19. B	
10. D		20. B	

21. C
22. D
23. B
24. D
25. A

SOLUTIONS TO PROBLEMS

1. Since the number of weekly inspections ranged from 20 to 40, this implies that the average weekly number of inspections never fell below 20 (choice B).

2. 591 ÷ .194 ≈ 3046, closest to 3000 students

3. (591-268) ÷ 268 ≈ 120%

4. Total processing cost = (268)($28)+(1688)($21) = $42,952, closest to $40,000. [Note: Since 268 represents 13.7%, total freshman population = 268 ÷ .137 ≈ 1956. Then, 1956 - 268 = 1688]

5. Let x = staff size in 2004-2005. Then, .80x = staff size in 2005-2006. Since the 2005-2006 staff produced 20% more work, this is represented by 1.20. However, to measure the productivity per staff member, the factor 1/.80 = 1.25 must also be used to equate the 2 staffs. Then, (1.20)(1.25) = 1.50. Thus, the 2005-2006 staff produced 50% more work than the 2004-2005 staff.

6. The respective percent increases are ≈ 20%, 17%, 39%, 29%. The largest would be, over the previous fiscal year, for the current fiscal year 2005-2006.

7. $\frac{P}{c}$ = number of buses needed per hour. If t = time (in hrs.), then $U_t = tP/c$

8. a = (2)(9) = 18 for 1 stop. Then, 288 ÷ 18 = 16 stops

9. 560 ÷ .35 = 1600 grand larcenies

10. 456 ÷ .226 ≈ 2018; 560 ÷ .35 = 1600. Then, (1600-2018) ÷ 2018 ≈ -20%, or a 20% decrease

11. $(\frac{1}{6})$(560) = $93\frac{1}{3}$. Then, $93\frac{1}{3}$ ÷ 1600 ≈ 5.8%

12. There are 5000 brake jobs and 3000 front-end jobs in one year. 5000 ÷ 4 = 1250 days, and 1250 ÷ 240 ≈ 5.2. Also, 3000 ÷ 3 = 1000 days, and 1000 ÷ 240 ≈ 4.2. Total number of workers needed ≈ 5.2 + 4.2 ≈ 10

13. (.94)(1.05)(1.10) = 1.0857, which represents an overall increase by about 8.6%

14. Average annual % change = $(1+TC)^{\frac{1}{3}}$ - 1 = $(1.0857)^{\frac{1}{3}}$ - 1 ≈ 2.8%

15. 357 ÷ .06 = 5950

16. In 2003, $(h)(1 - \frac{k}{100})$ pieces cost $(x)(1 + \frac{g}{100})$ dollars. To calculate the cost for 1 piece (average cost), find the value of $[(x)(1 + \frac{g}{100})] \div [(n)(1 - \frac{k}{100})] = [(x)(100+g)/100] \cdot [100/\{n(100-k)\}] = [x(100+g)]/[n(100-k)]$

17.

	#	Deductions Up To 50,000		
40,000	6	2000	3000	40,000-3,000-2,000 = 35,000 × 6
80,000	10	2000	2000	80,000-2,000-2,000 = 75,000 × 10
120,000	2	2000		118000 × 2

```
35,000 × 6 = 210,000  = 210
76,000 × 10 = 760,000  = 760
118,000 × 2 = 236,000  = 236
                        1206
```

1206 ÷ 18 = 67

18.

2002		Deductions		
40,000	2	2000	3000	35,000 × 2 = 70,000
80,000	11	2000	2000	76,000 × 11 = 836,000
120,000	5	2000		118,000 × 5 = 590,000
				1496,000

1,496,000 ÷ 18 = 83,111
83,111 - 67,000 = 16,111 = most nearly 16 (in thousands)

19. We are actually looking for the number of different groups of different sizes involving S. This reduces to $_4C_1 + _4C_2 + _4C_3 + _4C_4 = 4 + 6 + 4 + 1 = 15$. The notation $_nC_r$ means combinations of n things taken R at a time = $[(n)(n-1)(n-2)(\ldots)(n-R+1)]/[(R)(R-1)(\ldots)(1)]$. The 15 groups are: SA, SB, SC, SD, SAB, SAC, SAD, SBC, SBD, SCD, SABC, SABD, SACD, SBCD, SABCD.

20. Let x = total premiums. Then, $\frac{.93}{100} = \frac{x}{8,765,000}$
    Solving, x ≈ $81,515

21. The balance, raised from property taxes, = $3,240,000,000 - $1,100,000,000 - $121,600,000 = $2,018,400,000. Now, (.60)($42,500,000,000) = $25,500,000. The tax rate per $100 of assessed value = ($2,018,400,000)($100)/$25,500,000,000 ≈ $7.90

22. A dozen costs $(\$12.90)(\frac{12}{3}) = \$51.60$

23. $(40)(20) \div 8 = 100$ ft.

24. Total number of wrong-color files = (200)(.75)(.20)+(100)(.75)(.40) = 60

25. Total number of inspections = $(12)(4\frac{1}{2})+(20)(4\frac{1}{2})+(9)(2\frac{1}{2})+(4\frac{1}{2})(2)$ = 175.5   Closest entry is choice A.

CLERICAL ABILITIES TEST

EXAMINATION SECTION
TEST 1

DIRECTIONS: Each question or incomplete statement is followed by several suggested answers or completions. Select the one that *BEST* answers the question or completes the statement. *PRINT THE LETTER OF THE CORRECT ANSWER IN THE SPACE AT THE RIGHT.*

Questions 1-10.

DIRECTIONS: Questions 1 through 10 consist of lines of names, dates and numbers. For each question, you are to choose the option (A, B, C, or D) in Column II which *EXACTLY* matches the information in Column I. *PRINT THE LETTER OF THE CORRECT ANSWER IN THE SPACE AT THE RIGHT.*

SAMPLE QUESTION

Column I	Column II
Schneider 11/16/75 581932	A. Schneider 11/16/75 518932
	B. Schneider 11/16/75 581932
	C. Schnieder 11/16/75 581932
	D. Shnieder 11/16/75 518932

The correct answer is B. Only option B shows the name, date and number exactly as they are in Column I. Option A has a mistake in the number. Option C has a mistake in the name. Option D has a mistake in the name and in the number. Now answer Questions 1 through 10 in the same manner.

Column I	Column II	
1. Johnston 12/26/74 659251	A. Johnson 12/23/74 659251 B. Johston 12/26/74 659251 C. Johnston 12/26/74 695251 D. Johnston 12/26/74 659251	1.____
2. Allison 1/26/75 9939256	A. Allison 1/26/75 9939256 B. Alisson 1/26/75 9939256 C. Allison 1/26/76 9399256 D. Allison 1/26/75 9993256	2.____
3. Farrell 2/12/75 361251	A. Farell 2/21/75 361251 B. Farrell 2/12/75 361251 C. Farrell 2/21/75 361251 D. Farrell 2/12/75 361151	3.____
4. Guerrero 4/28/72 105689	A. Guererro 4/28/72 105689 B. Guerrero 4/28/72 105986 C. Guerrero 4/28/72 105869 D. Guerrero 4/28/72 105689	4.____

5. McDonnell 6/05/73 478215

   A. McDonnell 6/15/73 478215
   B. McDonnell 6/05/73 478215
   C. McDonnell 6/05/73 472815
   D. MacDonell 6/05/73 478215

5._____

6. Shepard 3/31/71 075421

   A. Sheperd 3/31/71 075421
   B. Shepard 3/13/71 075421
   C. Shepard 3/31/71 075421
   D. Shepard 3/13/71 075241

6._____

7. Russell 4/01/69 031429

   A. Russell 4/01/69 031429
   B. Russell 4/10/69 034129
   C. Russell 4/10/69 031429
   D. Russell 4/01/69 034129

7._____

8. Phillips 10/16/68 961042

   A. Philipps 10/16/68 961042
   B. Phillips 10/16/68 960142
   C. Phillips 10/16/68 961042
   D. Philipps 10/16/68 916042

8._____

9. Campbell 11/21/72 624856

   A. Campbell 11/21/72 624856
   B. Campbell 11/21/72 624586
   C. Campbell 11/21/72 624686
   D. Campbel 11/21/72 624856

9._____

10. Patterson 9/18/71 76199176

   A. Patterson 9/18/72 76191976
   B. Patterson 9/18/71 76199176
   C. Patterson 9/18/72 76199176
   D. Patterson 9/18/71 76919176

10._____

Questions 11-15.

DIRECTIONS: Questions 11 through 15 consist of groups of numbers and letters which you are to compare. For each question, you are to choose the option (A, B, C, or D) in Column II which *EXACTLY* matches the group of numbers and letters given in Column I.

SAMPLE QUESTION

Column I
B92466

Column II
A. B92644
B. B94266
C. A92466
D. B92466

The correct answer is D. Only option D in Column II shows the group of numbers and letters *EXACTLY* as it appears in Column I. Now answer Questions 11 through 15 in the same manner.

Column I
11.   925AC5

Column II
A. 952CA5
B. 925AC5
C. 952AC5
D. 925CA6

12.   Y006925

A. Y060925
B. Y006295
C. Y006529
D. Y006925

13.   J236956

A. J236956
B. J326965
C. J239656
D. J932656

14.   AB6952

A. AB6952
B. AB9625
C. AB9652
D. AB6925

15.   X259361

A. X529361
B. X259631
C. X523961
D. X259361

Questions 16-25.

DIRECTIONS: Each of Questions 16 through 25 consists of three lines of code letters and three lines of numbers. The numbers on each line should correspond with the code letters on the same line in accordance with the table below.

Code Letter	S	V	W	A	Q	M	X	E	G	K
Corresponding Number	0	1	2	3	4	5	6	7	8	9

On some of the lines, an error exists in the coding. Compare the letters and numbers in each question carefully. If you find an error or errors on:

only *one* of the lines in the question, mark your answer A;

any *two* lines in the question, mark your answer B;

all *three* lines in the question, mark your answer C;

none of the lines in the question, mark your answer D.

SAMPLE QUESTION

WQGKSXG   2489068
XEKVQMA   6591453
KMAESXV   9527061

In the above example, the first line is correct since each code letter listed has the correct corresponding number. On the second line, an error exists because code letter E should have the number 7 instead of the number 5. On the third line an error exists because the code letter A should have the number 3 instead of the number 2. Since there are errors in two of the three lines, the correct answer is B. Now answer Questions 16 through 25 in the same manner.

16.   SWQEKGA   0247983   16._____
       KEAVSXM   9731065
       SSAXGKQ   0036894

17.   QAMKMVS   4259510   17._____
       MGGEASX   5897306
       KSWMKWS   9125920

18. WKXQWVE   2964217
     QKXXQVA   4966413
     AWMXGVS   3253810   18._____

19. GMMKASE   8559307
     AWVSKSW   3210902
     QAVSVGK   4310189   19._____

20. XGKQSMK   6894049
     QSVKEAS   4019730
     GSMXKMV   8057951   20._____

21. AEKMWSG   3195208
     MKQSVQK   5940149
     XGQAEVW   6843712   21._____

22. XGMKAVS   6858310
     SKMAWEQ   0953174
     GVMEQSA   8167403   22._____

23. VQSKAVE   1489317
     WQGKAEM   2489375
     MEGKAWQ   5689324   23._____

24. XMQVSKG   6541098
     QMEKEWS   4579720
     KMEVKGA   9571983   24._____

25. GKVAMEW   8912572
     AXMVKAE   3651937
     KWAGMAV   9238531   25._____

Questions 26-35.

DIRECTIONS: Each of Questions 26 through 35 consists of a column of figures. For each question, add the column of figures and choose the correct answer from the four choices given.

26.   5,665.43
     2,356.69
     6,447.24
     <u>7,239.65</u>   26._____

     A. 20,698.01   B. 21,709.01
     C. 21,718.01   D. 22,609.01

27.   817,209.55
     264,354.29
      82,368.76
     <u>849,964.89</u>   27._____

     A. 1,893,997.49   B. 1,989,988.39
     C. 2,009,077.39   D. 2,013,897,49

28.   156,366.89
     249,973.23
     823,229.49
     <u>56,869.45</u>

    A. 1,286,439.06   B. 1,287,521.06
    C. 1,297,539.06   D. 1,296,421.06

    28.____

29.   23,422.15
     149,696.24
     238,377.53
      86,289.79
     <u>505,544.63</u>

    A.   989,229.34   B.   999,879.34
    C. 1,003,330.34   D. 1,023,329.34

    29.____

30.   2,468,926.70
      656,842.28
       49,723.15
      <u>832,369.59</u>

    A. 3,218,061.72   B. 3,808,092.72
    C. 4,007,861.72   D. 4,818,192.72

    30.____

31.   524,201.52
    7,775,678.51
    8,345,299.63
   40,628,898.08
   <u>31,374,670.07</u>

    A. 88,646,647.81   B. 88,646,747.91
    C. 88,648,647.91   D. 88,648,747.81

    31.____

32.   6,824,829.40
     682,482.94
   5,542,015.27
     775,678.51
   <u>7,732,507.25</u>

    A. 21,557,513.37   B. 21,567,513.37
    C. 22,567,503.37   D. 22,567,513.37

    32.____

33. 22,109,405.58
   6,097,093.43
   5,050,073.99
   8,118,050.05
  <u>4,313,980.82</u>

    A. 45,688,593.87   B. 45,688,603.87
    C. 45,689,593.87   D. 45,689,603.87

    33.____

34. 79,324,114.19
   99,848,129.74
   43,331,653.31
   <u>41,610,207.14</u>

    34.____

A. 264,114,104.38	B. 264,114,114.38
C. 265,114,114.38	D. 265,214,104.38

35. 33,729,653.94
       5,959,342.58
      26,052,715.47
       4,452,669.52
       7,079,953.59

A. 76,374,334.10	B. 76,375,334.10
C. 77,274,335.10	D. 77,275,335.10

Questions 36-40.

DIRECTIONS: Each of Questions 36 through 40 consists of a single number in Column I and four options in Column II. For each question, you are to choose the option (A, B, C, or D) in Column II which *EXACTLY* matches the number in Column I.

SAMPLE QUESTION

Column I
5965121

Column II
A.   5956121
B.   5965121
C.   5966121
D.   5965211

The correct answer is B. Only option B shows the number *EXACTLY* as it appears in Column I. Now answer Questions 36 through 40 in the same manner.

Column I
36.   9643242

Column II
A.   9643242
B.   9462342
C.   9642442
D.   9463242

37.   3572477

A.   3752477
B.   3725477
C.   3572477
D.   3574277

38.   5276101

A.   5267101
B.   5726011
C.   5271601
D.   5276101

39.   4469329

A.   4496329
B.   4469329
C.   4496239
D.   4469239

40.   2326308

A.   2236308
B.   2233608
C.   2326308
D.   2323608

KEY (CORRECT ANSWERS)

1.	D	11.	B	21.	A	31.	D
2.	A	12.	D	22.	C	32.	A
3.	B	13.	A	23.	B	33.	B
4.	D	14.	A	24.	D	34.	A
5.	B	15.	D	25.	A	35.	C
6.	C	16.	D	26.	B	36.	A
7.	A	17.	C	27.	D	37.	C
8.	C	18.	A	28.	A	38.	D
9.	A	19.	D	29.	C	39.	B
10.	B	20.	B	30.	C	40.	C

TEST 2

Questions 1-5.

DIRECTIONS: Each of Questions 1 through 5 consists of a name and a dollar amount. In each question, the name and dollar amount in Column II should be an exact copy of the name and dollar amount in Column I. If there is:

a mistake only in the name, mark your answer A;
a mistake only in the dollar amount, mark your answer B;
a mistake in both the name and the dollar amount, mark your answer C;
no mistake in either the name or the dollar amount, mark your answer D.

SAMPLE QUESTION

Column I	Column II
George Peterson	George Petersson
$125.50	$125.50

Compare the name and dollar amount in Column II with the name and dollar amount in Column I. The name *Petersson* in Column II is spelled *Peterson* in Column I. The amount is the same in both columns. Since there is a mistake only in the name, the answer to the sample question is A.

Now answer Questions 1 through 5 in the same manner.

Column I	Column II	
1. Susanne Shultz $3440	Susanne Schultz $3440	1.____
2. Anibal P. Contrucci $2121.61	Anibel P. Contrucci $2112.61	2.____
3. Eugenio Mendoza $12.45	Eugenio Mendozza $12.45	3.____
4. Maurice Gluckstadt $4297	Maurice Gluckstadt $4297	4.____
5. John Pampellonne $4656.94	John Pammpellonne $4566.94	5.____

Questions 6-11.

DIRECTIONS: Each of Questions 6 through 11 consists of a set of names and addresses which you are to compare. In each question, the name and addresses in Column II should be an *EXACT* copy of the name and address in Column I. If there is:

a mistake only in the name, mark your answer A;
a mistake only in the address, mark your answer B;
a mistake in both the name and address, mark your answer C;
no mistake in either the name or address, mark your answer D.

SAMPLE QUESTION

Column I	Column II
Michael Filbert	Michael Filbert
456 Reade Street	645 Reade Street
New York, N.	New York, N . Y. 10013

Since there is a mistake only in the address (the street number should be 456 instead of 645), the answer to the sample question is B.

Now answer Questions 6 through 11 in the same manner.

Column I	Column II	
6. Hilda Goettelmann 55 Lenox Rd. Brooklyn, N. Y. 11226	Hilda Goettelman 55 Lenox Ave. Brooklyn, N. Y. 11226	6.____
7. Arthur Sherman 2522 Batchelder St. Brooklyn, N. Y. 11235	Arthur Sharman 2522 Batcheder St. Brooklyn, N. Y. 11253	7.____
8. Ralph Barnett 300 West 28 Street New York, New York 10001	Ralph Barnett 300 West 28 Street New York, New York 10001	8.____
9. George Goodwin 135 Palmer Avenue Staten Island, New York 10302	George Godwin 135 Palmer Avenue Staten Island, New York 10302	9.____
10. Alonso Ramirez 232 West 79 Street New York, N. Y. 10024	Alonso Ramirez 223 West 79 Street New York, N. Y. 10024	10.____
11. Cynthia Graham 149-35 83 Street Howard Beach, N. Y. 11414	Cynthia Graham 149-35 83 Street Howard Beach, N. Y. 11414	11.____

Questions 12-20.

DIRECTIONS: Questions 12 through 20 are problems in subtraction. For each question do the subtraction and select your answer from the four choices given.

12. 232,921.85
-179,587.68   12.____

    A. 52,433.17   B. 52,434.17
    C. 53,334.17   D. 53,343.17

13. 5,531,876.29
-3,897,158.36   13.____

    A. 1,634,717.93   B. 1,644,718.93
    C. 1,734,717.93   D. 1,734,718.93

14. 1,482,658.22
- 937,925.76   14.____

    A. 544,633.46   B. 544,732.46
    C. 545,632.46   D. 545,732.46

15. 937,828.17
-259,673.88   15.____

    A. 678,154.29   B. 679,154.29
    C. 688,155.39   D. 699,155.39

16. 760,412.38
    -263,465.95

    A. 496,046.43   B. 496,946.43
    C. 496,956.43   D. 497,046.43

17. 3,203,902.26
    -2,933,087.96

    A. 260,814.30   B. 269,824.30
    C. 270,814.30   D. 270,824.30

18. 1,023,468.71
    - 934,678.88

    A. 88,780.83   B. 88,789.83
    C. 88,880.83   D. 88,889.83

19. 831,549.47
    -772,814.78

    A. 58,734.69   B. 58,834.69
    C. 59,735,69   D. 59,834.69

20. 6,306,281.74
    -3,617,376.75

    A. 2,687,904.99   B. 2,688,904.99
    C. 2,689,804.99   D. 2,799,905.99

Questions 21-30.

DIRECTIONS: Each of Questions 21 through 30 consists of three lines of code letters and three lines of numbers. The numbers on each line should correspond with the code letters on the same line in accordance with the table below.

Code Letter	J	U	B	T	Y	D	K	R	L	P
Corresponding Number	0	1	2	3	4	5	6	7	8	9

On some of the lines, an error exists in the coding. Compare the letters and numbers in each question carefully. If you find an error or errors on:
   only *one* of the lines in the question, mark your answer A;
   any *two* lines in the question, mark your answer B;
   all *three* lines in the question, mark your answer C;
   none of the lines in the question, mark your answer D.

SAMPLE QUESTION

BJRPYUR   2079417
DTBPYKJ   5328460
YKLDBLT   4685283

In the above sample the first line is correct since each code letter listed has the correct corresponding number. On the second line, an error exists because code letter P should have the number 9 instead of the number 8. The third line is correct since each code letter listed has the correct corresponding number. Since there is an error in *one* of the three lines, the correct answer is A.

Now answer Questions 21 through 30 in the same manner.

21. BYPDTJL 2495308   21.____
    PLRDTJU 9815301
    DTJRYLK 5207486

22. RPBYRJK 7934706   22.____
    PKTYLBU 9624821
    KDLPJYR 6489047

23. TPYBUJR 3942107   23.____
    BYRKPTU 2476931
    DUKPYDL 5169458

24. KBYDLPL 6345898   24.____
    BLRKBRU 2876261
    JTULDYB 0318542

25. LDPYDKR 8594567   25.____
    BDKDRJL 2565708
    BDRPLUJ 2679810

26. PLRLBPU 9858291   26.____
    LPYKRDJ 8936750
    TDKPDTR 3569527

27. RKURPBY 7617924   27.____
    RYUKPTJ 7426930
    RTKPTJD 7369305

28. DYKPBJT 5469203   28.____
    KLPJBTL 6890238
    TKPLBJP 3698209

29. BTPRJYL 2397148   29.____
    LDKUTYR 8561347
    YDBLRPJ 4528190

30. ULPBKYT 1892643   30.____
    KPDTRBJ 6953720
    YLKJPTB 4860932

KEY (CORRECT ANSWERS)

1.	A		16.	B
2.	C		17.	C
3.	A		18.	B
4.	D		19.	A
5.	C		20.	B
6.	C		21.	B
7.	C		22.	C
8.	D		23.	D
9.	A		24.	B
10.	B		25.	A
11.	D		26.	C
12.	C		27.	A
13.	A		28.	D
14.	B		29.	B
15.	A		30.	D

———

CODING
EXAMINATION SECTION

COMMENTARY

An ingenious question-type called coding, involving elements of alphabetizing, filing, name and number comparison, and evaluative judgment and application, has currently won wide acceptance in testing circles for measuring clerical aptitude and general ability, particularly on the senior (middle) grades (levels).

While the directions for this question-type usually vary in detail, the candidate is generally asked to consider groups of names, codes, and numbers, and, then, according to a given plan, to arrange codes in alphabetic order; to arrange these in numerical sequence; to re-arrange columns of names and numbers in correct order; to espy errors in coding; to choose the correct coding arrangement in consonance with the given directions and examples, etc.

This question-type appears to have few parameters in respect to form, substance, or degree of difficulty.

Accordingly, acquaintance with, and practice in the coding question is recommended for the serious candidate.

CODING

EXAMINATION SECTION
TEST 1

DIRECTIONS: Column I consists of serial numbers of dollar bills. Column II shows different ways of arranging the corresponding serial numbers.
The serial numbers of dollar bills in Column I begin and end with a capital letter and have an eight-digit number in between. The serial numbers in Column I are to be arranged according to the following rules:

First: In alphabetical order according to the first letter.

Second: When two or more serial numbers have the same first letter, in alphabetical order according to the last letter.

Third: When two or more serial numbers have the same first *and* last letters, in numerical order, beginning with the lowest number

The serial numbers in Column I are numbered (1) through (5) in the order in which they are listed. In Column II the numbers (1) through (5) are arranged in four different ways to show different arrangements of the corresponding serial numbers. Choose the answer in Column II in which the serial numbers are arranged according to the above rules.

SAMPLE QUESTION:

Column I		Column II	
1.	E75044127B	A.	4, 1, 3, 2, 5
2.	B96399104A	B.	4, 1, 2, 3, 5
3.	B93939086A	C.	4, 3, 2, 5, 1
4.	B47064465H	D.	3, 2, 5, 4, 1

In the sample question, the four serial numbers starting with B should be put before the serial number starting with E. The serial numbers starting with B and ending with A should be put before the serial number starting with B and ending with H. The three serial numbers starting with B and ending with A should be listed in numerical order, beginning with the lowest number. The correct way to arrange the serial numbers therefore is:

3.	B93939086A
2.	B96399104A
5.	B99040922A
4.	B47064465H
1.	E75044127B

Since the order of arrangement is 3, 2, 5, 4, 1, the answer to the sample question is D.

1.
1.	D89143888P	A.	3, 5, 2, 1, 4
2.	D98143838B	B.	3, 1, 4, 5, 2
3.	D89113883B	C.	4, 2, 3, 1, 5
4.	D89148338P	D.	4, 1, 3, 5, 2
5.	D89148388B		

1.____

	Column I		Column II		

2. 1. W62455599E
    2. W62455090F
    3. W62405099E
    4. V62455097F
    5. V62405979E

A. 2, 4, 3, 1, 5
B. 3, 1, 5, 2, 4
C. 5, 3, 1, 4, 2
D. 5, 4, 3, 1, 2

2.____

3. 1. N74663826M
    2. M74633286M
    3. N76633228N
    4. M76483686N
    5. M74636688M

A. 2, 4, 5, 3, 1
B. 2, 5, 4, 1, 3
C. 1, 2, 5, 3, 4
D. 2, 5, 1, 4, 3

3.____

4. 1. P97560324B
    2. R97663024B
    3. P97503024E
    4. R97563240E
    5. P97652304B

A. 1, 5, 2, 3, 4
B. 3, 1, 4, 5, 2
C. 1, 5, 3, 2, 4
D. 1, 5; 2* 3, 4

4.____

5. 1. H92411165G
    2. A92141465G
    3. H92141165C
    4. H92444165C
    5. A92411465G

A. 2, 5, 3, 4, 1
B. 3, 4, 2, 5, 1
C. 3, 2, 1, 5, 4
D. 3, 1, 2, 5, 4

5.____

6. 1. X90637799S
    2. N90037696S
    3. Y90677369B
    4. X09677693B
    5. M09673699S

A. 4, 3, 5, 2, 1
B. 5, 4, 2, 1, 3
C. 5, 2, 4, 1, 3
D. 5, 2, 3, 4, 1

6.____

7. 1. K78425174L
    2. K78452714C
    3. K78547214N
    4. K78442774C
    5. K78547724M

A. 4, 2, 1, 3, 5
B. 2, 3, 5, 4, 1
C. 1, 4, 2, 3, 5
D. 4, 2, 1, 5, 3

7.____

8. 1. P18736652U
    2. P18766352V
    3. T17686532U
    4. T17865523U
    5. P18675332V

A. 1, 3, 4, 5, 2
B. 1, 5, 2, 3, 4
C. 3, 4, 5, 1, 2
D. 5, 2, 1, 3, 4

8.____

9. 1. L51138101K
    2. S51138001R
    3. S51188111K
    4. S51183110R
    5. L51188100R

A. 1, 5, 3, 2, 4
B. 1, 3, 5, 2, 4
C. 1, 5, 2, 4, 3
D. 2, 5, 1, 4, 3

9.____

	Column I		Column II	

10.
1. J28475336D   A. 5, 1, 2, 3, 4   10.____
2. T28775363D   B. 4, 3, 5, 1, 2
3. J27843566P   C. 1, 5, 2, 4, 3
4. T27834563P   D. 5, 1, 3, 2, 4
5. J28435536D

11.
1. S55126179E   A. 1, 5, 2, 3, 4   11.____
2. R55136177Q   B. 3, 4, 1, 5, 2
3. P55126177R   C. 3, 5, 2, 1, 4
4. S55126178R   D. 4, 3, 1, 5, 2
5. R55126180P

12.
1. T64217813Q   A. 4, 1, 3, 2, 5   12.____
2. 1642178170   B. 2, 4, 3, 1, 5
3. T642178180   C. 4, 1, 5, 2, 3
4. I64217811Q   D. 2, 3, 4, 1, 5
5. T64217816Q

13.
1. B33886897B   A. 5, 1, 3, 4, 2   13.____
2. B38386882B   B. 1, 2, 5, 3, 4
3. D33389862B   C. 1, 2, 5, 4, 3
4. D33336887D   D. 2, 1, 4, 5, 3
5. B38888697D

14.
1. E11664554M   A. 4, 1, 2, 5, 3   14.____
2. F11164544M   B. 2, 4, 1, 5, 3
3. F11614455N   C. 4, 2, 1, 3, 5
4. E11665454M   D. 1, 4, 2, 3, 5
5. F16161545N

15.
1. C86611355W   A. 2, 4, 1, 5, 3   15.____
2. C68631533V   B. 1, 2, 4, 3, 5
3. G88633331W   C. 1, 2, 5, 4, 3
4. C68833515V   D. 1, 2, 4, 3, 5
5. G68833511W

16.
1. R73665312J   A. 3, 2, 1, 4, 5   16.____
2. P73685512J   B. 2, 3, 5, 1, 4
3. P73968511J   C. 2, 3, 1, 5, 4
4. R73665321K   D. 3, 1, 5, 2, 4
5. R63985211K

17.
1. X33661222U   A. 1, 4, 5, 2, 3   17.____
2. Y83961323V   B. 4, 5, 1, 3, 2
3. Y88991123V   C. 4, 5, 1, 2, 3
4. X33691233U   D. 4, 1, 5, 2, 3
5. X38691333U

	Column I		Column II	

18.
1. B22838847W   A. 4, 5, 2, 3, 1   18.____
2. B28833874V   B. 4, 2, 5, 1, 3
3. B22288344X   C. 4, 5, 2, 1, 3
4. B28238374V   D. 4, 1, 5, 2, 3
5. B28883347V

19.
1. H44477447G   A. 1, 3, 5, 4, 2   19.____
2. H47444777G   B. 3, 1, 5, 2, 4
3. H74777477C   C. 1, 4, 2, 3, 5
4. H44747447G   D. 3, 5, 1, 4, 2
5. H77747447C

20.
1. G11143447G   A. 3, 5, 1, 4, 2   20.____
2. G15133388C   B. 1, 4, 3, 2, 5
3. C15134378G   C. 5, 3, 4, 2, 1
4. G11534477C   D. 4, 3, 1, 2, 5
5. C15533337C

21.
1. J96693369F   A. 4, 3, 2, 5, 1   21.____
2. J66939339F   B. 2, 5, 4, 1, 3
3. J96693693E   C. 2, 5, 4, 3, 1
4. J96663933E   D. 3, 4, 5, 2, 1
5. J69639363F

22.
1. L15567834Z   A. 3, 1, 5, 2, 4   22.____
2. P11587638Z   B. 1, 3, 5, 4, 2
3. M51567688Z   C. 1, 3, 5, 2, 4
4. 055578784Z   D. 3, 1, 5, 4, 2
5. N53588783Z

23.
1. C83261824G   A. 2, 4, 1, 5, 3   23.____
2. C78361833C   B. 4, 2, 1, 3, 5
3. G83261732G   C. 3, 1, 5, 2, 4
4. C88261823C   D. 2, 3, 5, 1, 4
5. G83261743C

24.
1. A11710107H   A. 2, 1, 4, 3, 5   24.____
2. H17110017A   B. 3, 1, 5, 2, 4
3. A11170707A   C. 3, 4, 1, 5, 2
4. H17170171H   D. 3, 5, 1, 2, 4
5. A11710177A

25.
1. R26794821S   A. 3, 2, 4, 1, 5   25.____
2. 026794821T   B. 3, 4, 2, 1, 5
3. M26794827Z   C. 4, 2, 1, 3, 5
4. Q26794821R   D. 5, 4, 1, 2, 3
5. S26794821P

KEY (CORRECT ANSWERS)

1.	A		11.	C
2.	D		12.	B
3.	B		13.	B
4.	C		14.	D
5.	A		15.	A
6.	C		16.	C
7.	D		17.	A
8.	B		18.	B
9.	A		19.	D
10.	D		20.	C

21.	A
22.	B
23.	A
24.	D
25.	A

————

TEST 2

DIRECTIONS : Questions 1 through 5 consist of a set of letters and numbers located under Column I. For each question, pick the answer (A, B, C, or D) located under Column II which contains *ONLY* letters and numbers that appear in the question in Column 1. *PRINT THE LETTER OF THE CORRECT ANSWER IN THE SPACE AT THE RIGHT.*

SAMPLE QUESTION

Column I

B-9-P-H-2-Z-N-8-4-M

Column II

A.   B-4-C-3-R-9
B.   4-H-P-8-6-N
C.   P-2-Z-8-M-9
D.   4-B-N-5-E-Z

Choice C is the correct answer because P,2,Z,8,M and 9 all appear in the sample question. All the other choices have at least one letter or number that is not in the question.

Column I

1.   1-7-6-J-L-T-3-S-A-2

Column I

A.   J-3-S-A-7-L
B.   T-S-A-2-6-5
C.   3-7-J-L-S-Z
D.   A-7-4-J-L-1

1.____

2.   C-0-Q-5-3-9-H-L-2-7

A.   5-9-T-2-7-Q
B.   3-0-6-9-L-C
C.   9-L-7-Q-C-3
D.   H-Q-4-5-9-7

2.____

3.   P-3-B-C-5-6-0-E-1-T

A.   B-4-6-1-3-T
B.   T-B-P-3-E-0
C.   5-3-0-E-B-G
D.   0-6-P-T-9-B

3.____

4.   U-T-Z-2-4-S-8-6-B-3

A.   2-4-S-V-Z-3
B.   B-Z-S-8-3-6
C.   4-T-U-8-L-B
D.   8-3-T-Z-1-2

4.____

5.   4-D-F-G-C-6-8-3-J-L

A.   T-D-6-8-4-J
B.   C-4-3-2-J-F
C.   8-3-C-5-G-6
D.   C-8-6-J-G-L

5.____

Questions 6 - 12.

DIRECTIONS: Each of the questions numbered 11 through 17 consists of a long series of letters and numbers under Column I and four short series of letters and numbers under Column 11. Por each question, choose the short series of letters and numbers which is entirely and exactly the same as some part of the long series.

SAMPLE QUESTION:

Column I   Column II

JG13572XY89WB14

           A.   1372Y8
           B.   XYWB14
           C.   72XY89
           D.   J13572

In each of choices A, B, and D, one or more of the letters and numbers in the series in Column I is omitted. Only option C reproduces a segment of the series entirely and exactly. Therefore, C is the CORRECT answer to the sample question.

6.   IE227FE383L4700   A.   E27FE3   6._____
                                  B.   EF838L
                                  C.   EL4700
                                  D.   83L470

7.   77J646G54NPB318   A.   NPB318   7._____
                                  B.   J646J5
                                  C.   4G54NP
                                  D.   C54NPB

8.   85887T358W24A93   A.   858887   8._____
                                  B.   W24A93
                                  C.   858W24
                                  D.   87T353

9.   E104RY796B33H14   A.   04RY79   9._____
                                  B.   E14RYR
                                  C.   96B3H1
                                  D.   RY7996

10.   W58NP12141DE07M   A.   8MP121   10._____
                                  B.   W58NP1
                                  C.   14DEO7
                                  D.   12141D

11.   P473R365M442V5W   A.   P47365   11._____
                                  B.   73P365
                                  C.   365M44
                                  D.   5X42V5

12.　865CG441V21SS59

    A.　1V12SS
    B.　V21SS5
    C.　5GC441
    D.　894CG4

12.____

KEY (CORRECT ANSWERS)

1.	A	7.	A
2.	C	8.	B
3.	B	9.	A
4.	B	10.	D
5.	D	11.	C
6.	D	12.	B

TEST 3

SAMPLE :   B-9-P-H-2-Z-N-8-4-M

A.   B-4-C-3-E-9
B.   4-H-P-8-6-N
C.   P-2-Z-8-M-9
D.   4-B-N-5-E-2

Choice C is the correct answer because P, 2, Z, 8, M, 9 are in the sample question. All the other choices have at least one letter or number that is not in the question.

Questions 1 through 4 are based on Column I.

Column I

1. X-8-3-I-H-9-4-G-P-U   A.   I-G-W-8-2-1   1._____

2. 4-1-2-X-U-B-9-H-7-3   B.   U-3-G-9-P-8   2._____

3. U-I-G-2-5-4-W-P-3-B   C.   3-G-I-4-S-U   3._____

4. 3-H-7-G-4-5-I-U-8   D.   9-X-4-7-2-H   4._____

Questions 5 through 8 are based on Column II.

Column II

5. L-2-9-Z-R-8-Q-Y-5-7   A.   8-R-N-3-T-Z   5._____

6. J-L-9-N-Y-8-5-Q-Z-2   B.   2-L-R-5-7-Q   6._____

7. T-Y-3-3-J-Q-2-N-R-Z   C.   J-2-8-Z-Y-5   7._____

8. 8-Z-7-T-N-L-1-E-R-3   D.   Z-8-9-3-L-5   8._____

KEY (CORRECT ANSWERS)

1.	B		5.	B
2.	D		6.	C
3.	C		7.	A
4.	C		8.	A

———

TEST 4

DIRECTIONS : Questions 1 through 5 have lines of letters and numbers. Each letter should be matched with its number in accordance with the following table:

Letter	F	R	C	A	W	L	E	N	B	T
Matching Number	0	1	2	3	4	5	6	7	8	9

From the table you can determine that the letter F has the matching number 0 below it, the letter R has the matching number 1 below it, etc.

For each question, compare each line of letters and numbers carefully to see if each letter has its correct matching number. If all the letters and numbers are matched correctly in

    none of the lines of the question, mark your answer A
    only *one* of the lines of the question, mark your answer B
    only *two* of the lines of the question, mark your answer C
    all three lines of the question, mark your answer D

WBCR	4826
TLBF	9580
ATNE	3986

There is a mistake in the first line because the letter R should have its matching number 1 instead of the number 6. The second line is correct because each letter shown has the correct matching number.

There is a mistake in the third line because the letter N should have the matching number 7 instead of the number 8. Since all the letters and numbers are matched correctly in only one of the lines in the sample, the correct answer is B.

1.   EBCT   6829   1._____
            ATWR   3961
            NLBW   7584

2.   RNCT   1729   2._____
            LNCR   5728
            WAEB   5368

3.   STWB   7948   3._____
            RABL   1385
            TAEF   9360

4.   LWRB   5417   4._____
            RLWN   1647
            CBWA   2843

5.   ABTC   3792
            WCER   5261
            AWCN   3417

KEY (CORRECT ANSWERS)

1. C
2. B
3. D
4. B
5. A

———

TEST 5

DIRECTIONS : Assume that each of the capital letters in the table below represents the name of an employee enrolled in the city employees retirement system. The number directly beneath the letter represents the agency for which the employee works, and the small letter directly beneath represents the code for the employees account.

Name of Employee	L	O	T	Q	A	M	R	N	C
Agency	3	4	5	9	8	7	2	1	6
Account Code	r	f	b	i	d	t	g	e	n

In each of the following Questions 1 through 10, the agency code numbers and the account code letters in Columns 2 and 3 should correspond to the capital letters in Column 1 and should be in the same consecutive order. For each question, look at each column carefully and mark your answer as follows:

If there are one or more errors in *Column 2 only,* mark your answer *A,*

If there are one or more errors in *Column 3 only,* mark your answer B.

If there are one or more errors in Column 2 *and* one or more errors in Column 3, mark your answer C.

If there are *NO* errors in either column, mark your answer D,

The following sample question is given to help you understand the procedure.

Column 1	Column 2	Column 3
T Q L M O C	5 8 3 7 4 6	b i r t f n

In Column 2, the second agency code number (corresponding to letter Q) should be "9", not "8". Column 3 is coded correctly to Column 1. Since there is an error only in Column 2, the correct answer is A.

	Column 1	Column 2	Column 3	
1.	Q L N R C A	9 3 1 2 6 8	i f e g n d	1.____
2.	N R M O T C	1 2 7 5 4 6	e g f t b n	2.____
3.	R C T A L M	2 6 5 8 3 7	g n d b r t	3.____
4.	T A M L O N	5 7 8 3 4 1	b d t r f e	4.____
5.	A N T O R M	8 1 5 4 2 7	d e b i g t	5.____
6.	M R A L O N	7 2 8 3 4 1	t g d r f e	6.____
7.	C T N Q R O	6 5 7 9 2 4	n d e i g f	7.____
8.	Q M R O T A	9 7 2 4 5 8	i t g f b d	8.____
9.	R Q M C O L	2 9 7 4 6 3	g i t n f r	9.____
10.	N O M R T Q	1 4 7 2 5 9	e f t g b i	10.____

KEY (CORRECT ANSWERS)

1.	D	6.	D
2.	C	7.	C
3.	B	8.	D
4.	A	9.	A
5.	B	10.	D

———

TEST 6

DIRECTIONS: Each of Questions 1 through 6 consists of three lines of code letters and numbers. The numbers on each line should correspond to the code letters on the same line in accordance with the table below.

Code Letter	D	Y	K	L	P	U	S	R	A	E
Corresponding Number	0	1	2	3	4	5	6	7	8	9

On some of the lines an error exists in the coding. Compare the letters and numbers in each question carefully. If you find an error or errors on

only *one* of the lines in the question, mark your answer A;
any *two* lines in the question, mark your answer B;
all *three* lines in the question, mark your answer C;
none of the lines in the question, mark your answer D.

SAMPLE QUESTION

KSRYELD	-	2671930
SAPUEKL	-	6845913
RYKADLP	-	5128034

In the above sample, the first line is correct since each code letter listed has the correct corresponding number. On the second line, an error exists because code letter K should have number 2 instead of number 1. On the third line, an error exists because the code letter R should have the number 7 instead of the number 5. Since there are errors on two of the three lines, the correct answer is B.

Now answer the following questions, using the same procedure.

1. YPUSRLD   -   1456730   1.____
    UPSAEDY   -   5648901
    PREYDKS   -   4791026

2. AERLPUS   -   8973456   2.____
    DKLYDPA   -   0231048
    UKLDREP   -   5230794

3. DAPUSLA   -   0845683   3.____
    YKLDLPS   -   1230356
    PUSKYDE   -   4562101

4. LRPUPDL   -   3745403   4.____
    SUPLEDR   -   6543907
    PKEYDLU   -   4291025

5. KEYDESR   -   2910967   5.____
    PRSALEY   -   4678391
    LSRAYSK   -   3687162

6. YESREYL   -   1967913   6.____
    PLPRAKY   -   4346821
    YLPSRDU   -   1346705

KEY (CORRECT ANSWERS)

1. A
2. D
3. C
4. A
5. B
6. A

———

BASIC FUNDAMENTALS OF BOOKKEEPING

CONTENTS

BASIC FUNDAMENTALS OF BOOKKEEPING

I. INTRODUCTION

Why keep records? If you are a typical small-business man, your answer to this question is probably, "Because the Government requires it!" And if the question comes in the middle of a busy day, you may add a few heartfelt words about the amount of time you have to spend on records--just for the Government.

Is it "just for the Government," though? True, regulations of various governmental agencies have greatly increased the record-keeping requirements of business. But this may be a good thing for the small-business man, overburdened though he is.

Many small-business managers don't recognize their book-keeping records for what they can really do. Their attitudes concerning these records are typified by one businessman who said, "Records only tell you what you have done in the past. It's too late to do anything about the past; I need to know what is going to happen in the future." However, the past can tell us much about what may happen in the future; and, certainly we can profit in the future from knowledge of our past mistakes.

These same managers may recognize that records are necessary in filing their tax returns, or that a banker requires financial information before he will lend money, but often their appreciation of their bookkeeping systems ends at this point. However, there are many ways in which the use of such information can help an owner manage his business more easily and profitably.

The small-business man is confronted with an endless array of problems and decisions every day. Sound decisions require an informed manager; and many management problems can be solved with the aid of the right bookkeeping information.

II. Requirements of a Good Record System

Of course, to get information that is really valuable to you--to get the right information--requires a good bookkeeping system. What are the characteristics of a good system? You want one that is simple and easy to understand, reliable, accurate, consistent, and one that will get the information to you promptly.

A simple, well-organized system of records, regularly kept up, can actually be a timesaver--by bringing order out of disorder. Furthermore, competition is very strong in today's business areas. A businessman needs to know almost on a day-to-day basis where his business stands profitwise, which lines of merchandise or services are the most or the least profitable, what his working-capital needs are, and many other details. He can get this information with reasonable certainty only if he has a good recordkeeping system--one that gives him all the information he needs.

In setting up a recordkeeping system that is tailored to your business, you will probably need the professional help of a competent accountant. And you may want to retain the services of an accountant or bookkeeper to maintain these records. But it is your job to learn to interpret this information and to use it effectively.

One of the reasons that many managers have misgivings about keeping records is that they don't understand them or know how they can be used. The owner or manager of a small business may be an expert in his line of business; however, he generally does not have a background in keeping records. So he is usually confused. What we will try to do in this discussion is to highlight the "why and what of bookkeeping." In so-doing, we aim to eliminate that confusion.

2

III. IMPORTANT BOOKKEEPING RECORDS

Today's managers should be familiar with the following book-keeping records:

Journal

Ledgers

Balance sheet

Income statement

Funds flow statement

Visual No. 1

We will discuss each of them in turn. In addition, a brief discussion of other supporting records will be made.

A. Bookkeeping Books

The journal, which accountants call "the book of original entry," is a chronological record of <u>all</u> business transactions engaged in by the firm. It is simply a financial diary. The ledgers, or "books of account," are more specialized records used to classify the journal entries according to like elements. For example, there would be a separate ledger account for cash entries, another for all sales, and still others for items such as accounts receivable, inventory, and loans. All transactions are first entered in the journal, and then posted in the appropriate ledger. The journal and ledgers are of minor importance to the manager in making decisions, but they play a vital role for the accountant or bookkeeper because the more important accounting statements such as the balance sheet and the income statement are derived from the journal and ledger entries.

B. Financial Reports

The two principal financial reports in most businesses are the balance sheet and the income statement. Up to about 25 or 30 years ago, the balance sheet was generally considered to be the most important financial statement. Until that time, it was generally used only as a basis for the extension of credit and bank loans, and very little thought was given to the information it offered that might be important in the operation and management of the business. Starting about 30 years ago, emphasis has gradually shifted to the income statement. Today the balance sheet and income statements are of equal importance, both to the accountant in financial reporting and to the manager faced with a multitude of administrative problems.

Essentially, the balance sheet shows what a business has, what it owes, and the investment of the owners in the business. It can be likened to a snapshot, showing the financial condition of the business at a certain point in time. The income statement, on the other hand, is a summary of business operations for a certain period--usually between two balance sheet dates. The income statement can be compared to a moving picture; it indicates the activity of a business over a certain period of time. In very general terms, the balance sheet tells you where you are, and the income statement tells you how you got there since the last time you had a balance sheet prepared.

Both the balance sheet and income statement can be long and complicated documents. Both accountants and management need some device that can highlight the critical financial information contained in these complex documents. Certain standard ratios or relationships between items on the financial statements have been developed that allow the interested parties to quickly determine important characteristics of the firm's activities. There are many relationships that might be important in a specific business that would not be as significant in another.

Other devices of the bookkeeper, such as funds flow statements, daily summaries of sales and cash receipts, the checkbook, account receivable records, property depreciation records, and insurance scheduling have also been found useful to management.

C. THE BALANCE SHEET

As stated earlier, the balance sheet represents what a business has, what it owes, and the investment of the owners. The things of value that the business has or owns are called assets. The claims of creditors against these assets are called liabilities. The value of the assets over and above the liabilities can be justifiably called the owner's claim. This amount is usually called the owner's equity (or net worth).

This brings us to the dual-aspect concept of bookkeeping. The balance sheet is set up to portray two aspects of each entry or event recorded on it. For each thing of value, or asset, there is a claim against that asset. The recognition of this concept leads to the balance sheet formula: ASSETS = LIABILITIES + OWNER'S EQUITY. Let's take an example to clarify this concept. Suppose Joe Smith decides to start a business. He has $2,000 cash in the bank. He got this sum by investing $1,000 of his own money and by borrowing $1,000 from the bank. If he were to draw up a balance sheet at this time, he would have assets of $2,000 cash balanced against a liability claim of $1,000 and an owner's claim of $1,000. Using the balance sheet

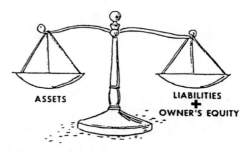

ASSETS = LIABILITIES + OWNER'S EQUITY

ASSETS   LIABILITIES
                 +
            OWNER'S EQUITY

Visual No. 2

formula: $2,000 = $1,000 + $1,000. This formula means there will always be a balance between assets and claims against them. The balance sheet always balances unless there has been a clerical error.

THE BLANK COMPANY
December 31, 196-

ASSETS

LIABILITIES

OWNER'S EQUITY

Visual No. 3

The balance sheet is usually constructed in a two-column format. The assets appear in the left hand column and the claims against the assets (the liabilities and owner's equity) are in the right hand column. Other formats are sometimes used; but, in any case, the balance sheet is an itemized or detailed account of the basic formula: assets = liabilities + owner's equity.

1. Assets

I have been speaking of assets belonging to the business. Of course, the business does not legally own anything unless it is organized as a corporation. But regardless of whether the business is organized as a proprietorship, a partnership, or a corporation, all business bookkeeping should be reckoned and accounted apart from the accounting of the personal funds and assets of its owners.

Assets are typically classified into three categories:

Current assets

Fixed assets

Other assets

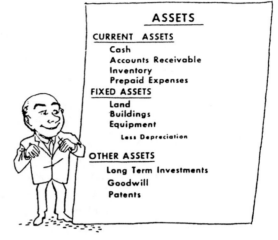

ASSETS

CURRENT ASSETS
Cash
Accounts Receivable
Inventory
Prepaid Expenses

FIXED ASSETS
Land
Buildings
Equipment
Less Depreciation

OTHER ASSETS
Long Term Investments
Goodwill
Patents

a. Current Assets

Visual No. 4

For bookkeeping purposes, the term "current assets" is used to designate cash and other assets which can be converted to cash during the normal operating cycle of the business (usually one year). The distinction between current assets and noncurrent assets is important since lenders and others pay much attention to the total amount of current assets. The size of current assets has a significant relationship to the stability of the business because it represents, to some degree, the amount of cash that might be raised quickly to meet current obligations. Here are some of the major current asset items.

Cash consists of funds that are immediately available to use without restrictions. These funds are usually in the form of checking-account deposits in banks, cash-register money, and petty cash. Cash should be large enough to meet obligations that are immediately due.

Accounts receivable are amounts owed to the company by its customers as a result of sales. Essentially, these accounts are the result of granting credit to customers. They may take the form of charge accounts where no interest or service charge is made, or they may be of an interest-bearing nature. In either case they are a drain on working capital. The more that is outstanding on accounts receivable, the less money that is available to meet current needs. The trick with accounts receivable is to keep them small enough so as not to endanger working capital, but large enough to keep from losing sales to credit-minded customers.

Inventory is defined as those items which are held for sale in the ordinary course of business, or which are to be consumed in the production of goods and services that are to be sold. Since accountants are conservative by nature, they include in inventory only items that are salable, and these items are valued at cost or market value, whichever is lower. Control of inventory and inventory expenses is one of management's most important jobs-- particularly for retailers--and good bookkeeping records in this area are particularly useful.

Prepaid expenses represent assets, paid for in advance, but whose usefulness will usually expire in a short time. A good example of this is prepaid insurance. A business pays for insurance protection in advance--usually three to five years in advance. The right to this protection is a thing of value--an asset--and the unused portion can be refunded or converted to cash.

b. Fixed Assets

"Fixed assets" are items owned by the business that have relatively long life. These assets are used in the production or sale of other goods and services. If they were held for resale, they would be classified as inventory, even though they might be long-lived assets.

Normally these assets are composed of land, buildings, and equipment. Some companies lump their fixed assets into one entry on their balance sheets, but you gain more information and can exercise more control over these assets if they are listed separately on the balance sheet. You may even want to list various types of equipment separately.

There is one other aspect of fixed-asset bookkeeping that we should discuss--and this is depreciation. Generally fixed assets--with the exception of land--depreciate, or decrease in value with the passing of time. That is, a building or piece of equipment that is five years old is not worth as much as it was when it was new. For a balance sheet to show the true value of these assets, it must reflect this loss in value. For both tax and other accounting purposes, the businessman is allowed to deduct this loss in value each year over the useful life of the assets, until, over a period of time, he has deducted the total cost of the asset. There are several accepted ways to calculate how much of an asset's value can be deducted for depreciation in a given year. This information and other facts concerning depreciation are discussed in Small Marketers Aid No. 68, <u>Depreciation Costs - Don't Overlook Them</u>, which is available free from the SBA. (See Supply Department.) Depreciation is allowed as an expense item on the income statement, and we will discuss this fact later.

c. <u>Other Assets</u>

"Other assets" is a miscellaneous category. It accounts for any investments of the firm in securities, such as stock in other private companies or government bonds. It also includes intangible assets such as goodwill, patents, and franchise costs. Items in the "other-assets" category have a longer life than current-asset items.

2. <u>Liabilities</u>

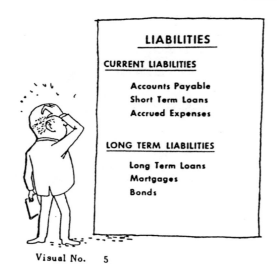

Visual No. 5

LIABILITIES

CURRENT LIABILITIES

Accounts Payable
Short Term Loans
Accrued Expenses

LONG TERM LIABILITIES

Long Term Loans
Mortgages
Bonds

"Liabilities" are the amounts of money owed by the business to people other than the owners. They are claims against the company's total assets, although they are not claims against any specific asset, except in the cases of some mortgages and equipment liens. Essentially, liabilities are divided into two classes:

Current liabilities

Long-term liabilities.

a. Current Liabilities

The term "current liabilities" is used to describe those claims of outsiders on the business that will fall due within one year. Here are some of the more important current-liabilities entries on the balance sheet:

Accounts payable represent the amounts owed to vendors, wholesalers, and other suppliers from whom the business has bought items on account. This includes any items of inventory, supply, or capital equipment which have been purchased on credit and for which payment is expected in less than one year. For example, a retail butcher purchased 500 pounds of meat for $250, a quantity of fish that cost $50, and a new air-conditioning unit for his store for $450. He bought all of these items on 60-day terms. His accounts payable were increased by $750. Of course, at the same time his inventory increased by $300 and his fixed assets rose by $450. If he had paid cash for these items, his accounts payable would not have been affected, but his cash account would have decreased by $750, thus keeping the accounting equation in balance.

Short-term loans, which are sometimes called notes payable, are loans from individuals, banks, or other lending institutions which fall due within a year. Also included in this category is the portion of any long-term debt that will come due within a year.

Accrued expenses are obligations which the company has incurred, but for which there has been no formal bill or invoice as yet. An example of this is accrued taxes. The owner knows the business has the obligation to pay taxes; and they are accruing or accumulating each day. The fact that the taxes do not have to be paid until a later date

9

does not diminish the obligation. Another example of accrued expenses is wages. Although wages are paid weekly or monthly, they are being earned hourly or daily and constitute a valid claim against the company. An accurate balance sheet will reflect these obligations.

b. Long-Term Liabilities

Claims of outsiders on the business that do not come due within one year are called "long-term liabilities" or, simply, "other liabilities." Included in this category are bonded indebtedness, mortgages, and long-term loans from individuals, banks, and others from whom the business may borrow money, such as the SBA. As was stated before, any part of a long-term debt that falls due within one year from the date of the balance sheet would be recorded as part of the current liabilities of the business.

Owner's Equity

The owner's equity section of the balance sheet is located on the right-hand side underneath the listing of the liabilities. It shows the claims of the owners on the company. Essentially, this is a balancing figure--that is, the owners get what's left of the assets after the liability claims have been recognized. This is an obvious definition, if you will remember the balance sheet formula. Transposing the formula as we learned it a few minutes ago, it becomes Assets - Liabilities = Owner's Equity. In the case where the business is a sole proprietorship, it is customary to show owner's equity as one entry with no distinction being made between the owner's initial investment and the accumulated retained earnings of the business. However, in the case of an incorporated business, there are entries for stockholders' claims as well as for earnings that have been accumulated and retained in the business. Of course, if the business has been consistently operating at a loss, the proprietor's claim may be less than his initial investment. And, in the case of a corporation, the balancing account could be operating deficit rather than retained earnings.

If we put together the entries we have been talking about, we have a complete balance sheet (such as the one shown in Visual No. 6 for the Blank Company). There is a lot of information in this statement. It tells you just what you have and where it is. It also tells you what you owe. You need this information to help you decide what actions you should take in running your business. If you need to borrow money, the banker or anyone else from whom you borrow will want to look at your balance sheet.

BALANCE SHEET
THE BLANK COMPANY
December 31, 196-

ASSETS			LIABILITIES	
CURRENT ASSETS				
Cash		$ 1,200	Accounts Payable	1,400
Accounts Receivable		2,500	Accrued Expenses	750
Inventory		2,500	Short Term Loans	1,000
FIXED ASSETS			Long Term Loan	3,000
			Mortgage	7,000
Land		3,000		
Building	15,000			
Equipment	2,500		**OWNER'S EQUITY**	
	17,500		John O. Blank	5,000
Less			Earned Surplus	1,050
Depreciation	5,500	12,000		
		$21,200		$21,200

Visual No. 6

D. THE INCOME STATEMENT

In recent years the income statement has become as important as the balance sheet as a financial and management record. It is also called the profit and loss statement, or simply the P and L statement. This financial record summarizes the activities of the company over a period of time, listing those that can be expressed in dollars. That is, it reports the revenues of the company and the expenses incurred in obtaining the revenues, and it shows the profit or loss resulting from these activities. The income statement complements the balance sheet. While balance sheet analysis shows the change in position of the company at the end of accounting periods, the income statement shows how the change took place during the accounting period. Both reports are necessary for a full understanding of the operation of the business.

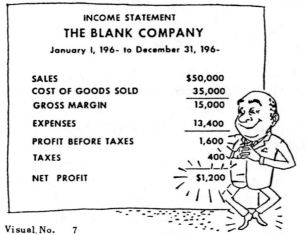

INCOME STATEMENT
THE BLANK COMPANY
January 1, 196- to December 31, 196-

SALES	$50,000
COST OF GOODS SOLD	35,000
GROSS MARGIN	15,000
EXPENSES	13,400
PROFIT BEFORE TAXES	1,600
TAXES	400
NET PROFIT	$1,200

Visual No. 7

The income statement for a particular company should be tailored to fit the activities of that company, and there is no rigid format that must be followed in constructing this report. But the following categories are found in most income statements.

11

1. Sales

The major activity of most businesses is the sales of products and services, and the bulk of revenue comes from sales. In recording sales, the figure used is net sales--that is, sales after discounts, allowances, and returned goods have been accounted for.

2. Cost of Goods Sold

Another important item, in calculating profit or loss, is the cost of the goods that the company has sold. This item is difficult to calculate accurately. Since the goods sold come from inventory, and since the company may have bought parts of its inventory at several prices, it is hard to determine exactly what is the cost of the particular part of the inventory that was sold. In large companies, and particularly in companies using cost accounting, there are some rather complicated methods of determining "cost of goods sold," but they are beyond the scope of this presentation. However, there is a simple, generally accepted way of calculating cost of goods sold. In this method you simply add the net amount of purchases during the accounting period to your beginning inventory, and subtract from this your ending inventory. The result can be considered cost-of-goods sold.

COST OF GOODS SOLD

BEGINNING INVENTORY	$ 2,400
PURCHASES	+ 35,100
GOODS AVAILABLE FOR SALE	= 37,500
ENDING INVENTORY	− 2,500
COST OF GOODS SOLD	= $35,000

Visual No. 8

3. Gross Margin

The difference between sales and cost of goods sold is called the "gross margin" or gross profit. This item is often expressed as a percentage of sales, as well as in dollar figures. The percentage gross margin is a very significant figure because it indicates what the average markup is on the merchandise sold. So, if a manager knows his expenses as a percentage of sales, he can calculate the markup necessary to obtain the gross margin he needs for a profitable operation. It is surprising how many small-business men do not know what basis to use in setting markups. In fact, with the various allowances, discounts, and markdowns that a business may offer, many managers do not know what their markup actually is. The gross margin calculation on the income statement can help the manager with this problem.

There are other costs of running a business besides the cost of the goods sold. When you use the simple method of determining costs of goods sold, these costs are called "expenses."

For example, here are some typical expenses: salaries and wages, utilities, depreciation, interest, administrative expenses, supplies, bad debts, advertising, and taxes--Federal, State, and local. These

EXPENSES	
SALARIES & WAGES	$5,500
UTILITIES	500
DEPRECIATION	875
INTEREST	600
INSURANCE	100
ADMINISTRATIVE EXPENSE	5,000
SUPPLIES	125
BAD DEBT EXPENSE	100
ADVERTISING	250
STATE, LOCAL & EXCISE TAXES	350
TOTAL EXPENSES	$13,400

Visual No. 9

are typical expenses, but there are many other kinds of expenses that may be experienced by other businesses. For example, we have shown in the Blank Company's balance sheet that he owns his own land and building--with a mortgage, of course. This accounts for part of his depreciation and interest expenses, but for a company that rents its quarters, rent would appear as the expense item. Other common expenses are traveling expense, commissions, and advertising.

Most of these expense items are self-explanatory, but there are a few that merit further comment. For one thing, the salary or draw of the owner should be recorded among the expenses--either as a part of salaries and wages or as part of administrative expenses. To exclude the owner's compensation from expenses distorts the actual profitability of the business. And, if the company is incorporated, it would reduce the allowable tax deductions of the business. Of course, for tax purposes, the owner's salary or draw in a proprietorship or partnership is considered as part of the net profit.

We discussed depreciation when we examined the balance sheet, and we mentioned that it was an item of expense. Although no money is actually paid out for depreciation, it is a real expense because it represents reduction in the value of the assets.

The most important thing about expenses is to be sure to include all of the expenses that the business incurs. This not only helps the owner get a more accurate picture of his operation but it allows him to take full advantage of the tax deductions that legitimate expenses offer.

13

4. Net Profit

In a typical company, when expenses are subtracted from gross margin, the remainder is profit. However, if the business receives revenue from sources other than sales, such as rents, dividends on securities held by the company, or interest on money loaned by the company, it is added to profit at this point. For bookkeeping purposes, the resulting profit is labeled "profit before taxes." This is the figure from which Federal income taxes are figured. If the business is a proprietorship, the profit is taxed as part of the owner's income. If the business is a corporation, the profits may be taxed on the basis of the corporate income tax schedule. When income taxes have been accounted for, the resultant entry is called "net profit after taxes," or simply "net profit." This is usually the final entry on the income statement.

Another financial record which managers can use to advantage is the funds flow statement. This statement is also called statement of sources and uses of funds and sometimes the "where got--where gone" statement. Whatever you call it, a record of sources and uses of past funds is useful to the manager. He can use it to evaluate past performance, and as a guide in determining future uses and sources of money.

When we speak of "funds" we do not necessarily mean actual "dollars" or "cash." Although accounting records are all written in monetary terms, they do not always involve an exchange of money. Many times in business transactions, it is credit rather than dollars that changes hands. Therefore, when we speak of funds flow, we are speaking of exchanges of <u>economic values</u> rather than merely the physical flow of dollars.

Basically, funds are used to: increase assets and reduce liabilities. They are also sometimes used to reduce owner's equity. An example of this would be the use of company funds to buy up outstanding stock or to buy out a partner. Where do funds come from? The three basic sources of funds are a reduction in assets, increases in liabilities, and increased owner's equity. All balance sheet items can be affected by the obtaining and spending of company funds.

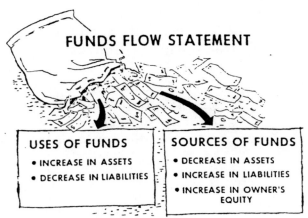

FUNDS FLOW STATEMENT

USES OF FUNDS	SOURCES OF FUNDS
• INCREASE IN ASSETS	• DECREASE IN ASSETS
• DECREASE IN LIABILITIES	• INCREASE IN LIABILITIES
	• INCREASE IN OWNER'S EQUITY

Visual No. 10

To examine the construction and use of a funds flow statement, let's take another look at the Blank Company. Here we show comparative balance sheets for two one-year periods (Visual No. 12). For the sake of simplicity, we have included only selected items from the balance sheets for analysis. Notice that the company gained funds by:

COMPARISON OF SELECTED BALANCE SHEET ITEMS
THE BLANK COMPANY

	LAST YEAR	THIS YEAR	SOURCE OF FUNDS	USE OF FUNDS
ASSETS				
CASH	1500	1200	300	
ACCOUNTS RECEIVABLE	2200	2500		300
INVENTORY	2300	2500		200
EQUIPMENT	2000	2500		500
LIABILITIES				
ACCOUNTS PAYABLE	1000	1400	400	
LONG TERM LOANS	5000	5000		
MORTGAGE	8000	7000		1000
OWNER'S EQUITY				
JOHN Q. BLANK	4500	5000	500	
EARNED SURPLUS	250	1050	800	

Visual No.   11

reducing cash $300,

increasing accounts payable $400,

putting $500 more owner's equity in the business, and

plowing back $800 of the profit into the business.

These funds were used to:

increase accounts receivable $300,

increase inventory $200,

buy $500 worth of equipment, and

pay off $1, 000 worth of long-term debt.

15

This funds flow statement has indicated to Mr. Blank where he has gotten his funds and how he has spent them. He can analyze these figures in the light of his plans and objectives and take appropriate action.

For example, if Mr. Blank wants to answer the question "Should I buy new capital equipment?" a look at his funds flow statement would show him his previous sources of funds, and it would give him a clue as to whether he could obtain funds for any new equipment.

IV. OTHER RECORDS

Up to this point, we have been talking about the basic types of bookkeeping records. In addition, we have discussed the two basic financial statements of a business: the balance sheet and the profit and loss statement. Now let us give our attention briefly to some other records which are very helpful to running a business successfully.

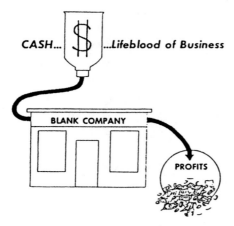

CASH... $ ...Lifeblood of Business

BLANK COMPANY

PROFITS

Visual No. 12

One element that appears on the balance sheet which I believe we can agree is important is cash. Because it is the lifeblood of all business, cash should be controlled and safeguarded at all times. The daily summary of sales and cash receipts and the checkbook are used by many managers of small businesses to help provide that control.

A. Daily Summary of Sales and Cash Receipts

Not all businesses summarize their daily transactions. However, a daily summary of sales and cash receipts is a very useful tool for checking how your business is doing on a day-to-day basis. At the close of each day's business, the actual cash on hand is counted and "balanced" against the total of the receipts recorded for the day. This balancing is done by means of the Daily Summary of Sales and Cash Receipts. (Handout No. 4-3). This is a recording of every cash receipt and every charge sale, whether you use a cash register or sales checks or both. If you have more than one cash register, a daily summary should be prepared for each; the individual cash-register summaries can then be combined into one overall summary for convenience in handling.

In the daily summary form used for purposes of illustration, (see Handout), the first section, "Cash Receipts," records the total of all cash taken in during the day from whatever source. This is the cash that must be accounted for over and above the amount in the change and/or petty cash funds. We shall touch upon these two funds later. The three components of cash receipts are (1) cash sales, (2) collections on accounts, and (3) miscellaneous receipts.

The daily total of cash sales is obtained from a cash-register tape reading or, if no cash register is used, by totaling the cash-sales checks.

For collections on accounts, an individual record of each customer payment on account should be kept, whether or not these collections are rung up on a cash register. The amount to be entered on the daily summary is obtained by totaling these individual records.

Miscellaneous receipts are daily cash transactions that cannot be classified as sales or collections. They might include refunds from suppliers for overpayment, advertising rebates or allowances, collections of rent from sub-leases or concessions, etc. Like collections on account, a sales check or memo should be made out each time such cash is taken in.

The total of daily cash receipts to be accounted for on the daily summary is obtained by adding cash sales, collections on account, and miscellaneous receipts.

The second section, "Cash on Hand," of a daily summary is a count of the cash actually on hand plus the cash that is represented by petty cash slips. The daily summary provides for counts of your total coins, bills, and checks as well as the amount expended for petty cash. The latter is determined by adding the amounts on the individual petty cash slips. By totaling all four of these counts, you obtain the total cash accounted for. To determine the amount of your daily cash deposit, you deduct from the "total cash accounted for" the total of the petty cash and change funds.

Cash to be deposited on the daily summary should always equal the total receipts to be accounted for minus the fixed amount of your petty cash and change funds. If it does not, all the work in preparing the daily summary should be carefully checked. Obviously, an error in giving change, in ringing up a sale, or neglecting to do so, will result in a cash shortage or overage. The daily summary provides spaces for such errors so that the proper entries can be made in your bookkeeping records. The last section of your daily summary, "Sales," records the total daily sales broken down into (1) cash sales and (2) charge sales.

As soon as possible after the daily summary has been completed, all cash for deposit should be taken to the bank. A duplicate deposit slip, stamped by the bank, should be kept with the daily summary as evidence that the deposit was made.

B. <u>Petty Cash and Charge Funds</u>

The record of daily sales and cash receipts which we have just described is designed on the assumption that a petty cash fund and a change cash fund, or a combination change and petty cash fund, are used. All businesses, small and large, have day-to-day expenses that are so small they do not warrant the drawing of a check. Good management practice calls for careful control of such expenses. The petty cash fund provides such control. It is a sum of money which is obtained by drawing a check to provide several day's, a week's, or a month's need of cash for small purchases. The type of business will determine the amount of the petty cash fund.

DOCUMENT YOUR PETTY CASH EXPENSES

Visual No. 13

Each time a payment is made from the petty cash, a slip should be made out. If an invoice or receipt is available, it should be attached to the petty-cash slip. The slips and the money ordinarily, but not necessarily, are kept separate from other currency in your cash till, drawer, or register. At all times, the total of unspent petty cash and petty cash slips should equal the fixed amount of the fund. When the total of the slips approaches the fixed amount of the petty cash fund, a check is drawn for the total amount of the slips. The money from this check is used to bring the fund back to its fixed amount.

In addition to a petty cash fund, some businesses that receive cash in over-the-counter transactions have a change fund. The amount needed for making change varies with the size and type of business, and, in some cases, with the days of the week. Control of the money in your change fund will be made easier, however, if you set a fixed amount large enough to meet all the ordinary change-making needs of your business. Each day, when the day's receipts are balanced and prepared for a bank deposit, you will retain bills and coins totaling the fixed amount of the fund for use the following day. Since you had that amount on hand before you made the day's first sale, the entire amount of the day's receipts will still be available for your bank deposit.

In some cases, the petty cash fund is kept in a petty cash box or safe, apart from the change fund. However, the same fund can serve for both petty cash and change. For example, if you decide that you need $50 for making change and $25 for petty cash, one $75 fund can be used. Whenever, in balancing the day's operations, you see that the petty cash slips total more than $25, you can write a petty cash check for the amount of the slips.

C. Record of Cash Disbursement

To safeguard your cash, it is recommended that all receipts be deposited in a bank account and that all disbursements, except those made from the petty cash fund, be made by drawing a check on that account. Your bank account should be used exclusively for business transactions. If your business is typical, you will have to write checks for merchandise purchases, employee's salaries, rent, utilities, payroll taxes, petty cash, and various other expenses. Your check stubs will serve as a record of cash disbursements.

The checkbook stub should contain all the details of the disbursement including the date, payee, amount and purpose of the payment. In addition, a running balance of the amount you have in your bank account should be maintained by subtracting the amount of each check from the existing balance after the previous check was drawn. If the checks of your checkbook are prenumbered, it is important to mark plainly in the stub when a check is voided for one reason or another.

Each check should have some sort of written document to support it--an invoice, petty-cash voucher, payroll summary and so on. Supporting documents should be approved by you or someone you have authorized before a check is drawn. They should be marked paid and filed after the check is drawn.

Periodically, your bank will send you a statement of your account and return cancelled checks for which money has been withdrawn from your account. It is important that you reconcile your records with those of the bank. This means that the balances in your checkbook and on the bank statement should agree. Uncashed checks must be deducted from your checkbook balance and deposits not recorded on the bank statement must be added to its balance in order to get both balances to agree.

D. Accounts Receivable Records

If you extend credit to your customers, you must keep an accurate account of your credit sales not only in total as you have done on the daily summary but also by the amount that each individual customer owes you. Moreover, you must be systematic about billings and collections. This is important. It results in better relations with your charge customers and in fewer losses from bad debts.

The simplest method of handling accounts receivable--other than just keeping a file of sales-slip carbons--is to have an account sheet for each credit customer. Charge sales and payments on charge sales are posted to each customer sheet. Monthly billing to each of your charge customers should be made from their individual account sheets.

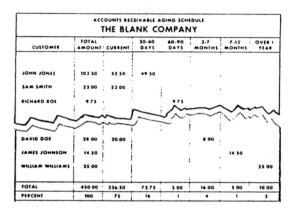

Visual No. 14

At least two or three times a year, your accounts receivable should be aged. You do this by posting each customer's account and his unpaid charges in columns according to age. These columns are labeled: not due; 1 to 30 days past due; 31 to 60 days past due; 61 to 90 days past due; etc. This analysis will indicate those customers who are not complying with your credit terms.

E. Property Records and Depreciation

In every type of business, it is necessary to purchase property and equipment from time to time. This property usually will last for several years, so it would be unrealistic to show the total amount of the purchase as an expense in any one year. Therefore, when this property is set up in the books as an asset, records must be kept to decrease its value over its life. This decrease is known as depreciation. I have mentioned this before during this talk. The amount of the decrease in value in one year, that is, the depreciation, is charged as an expense for the year.

I am talking about this expense, particularly, because no cash is paid out for it. It is a non-cash, not-out-of-pocket expense. You don't have to hand over actual money at the end of the month.

Records should be kept of this because, otherwise, there is a danger that this expense will be overlooked. Yet it is impossible to figure true profit or loss without considering it.

When you deduct the depreciation expense from your firm's income, you reduce your tax liabilities. When you put this depreciation expense into a depreciation allowance account, you are keeping score on your "debt" to depreciation.

In a barber shop, to take a simple example, depreciation of its chairs, dryers, and clippers at the end of the year amounts to $136. You deduct this $136 from the shop's income, in this case, to pay the debt credited to your depreciation allowance account. Since this equipment has the same depreciation value each year, the depreciation allowance account at the end of 3 years will show that a total of $408 worth of equipment has been used up. The books of the barbershop therefore show an expense of $408 which actually has not been spent. It is in the business to replace the depreciated equipment. If replacement will not take place in the immediate future, the money can be used in inventory, or in some other way to generate more sales or profits.

How you handle this money depends on many things. You can set it aside at a low interest rate and have that much less operating money. Or you can put it to work in your business where it will help to keep your finances healthy.

Remember, however, that you must be prepared financially when it is time to buy replacement equipment. A depreciation allowance account on your books can help to keep you aware of this. It helps you keep score on how much depreciation or replacement money you are using in your business.

Keeping score with a depreciation allowance account helps you to know when you need to convert some of your assets into replacement cash. If, for example, you know on January 1 that your delivery truck will be totally depreciated by June 30, you can review the situation objectively. You can decide whether you ought to use the truck longer or replace it. If you decide to replace it, then you can plan to accumulate the cash, and time the purchase in order to make the best deal.

F. Schedule of Insurance Coverage

The schedule of insurance coverage is prepared to indicate the type of coverage and the amount presently in force. This schedule should list all the insurance carried by your business--fire and extended coverage, theft, liability, life, business interruption and so forth.

This schedule should be prepared to present the following: name of insurance company, annual premium, expiration date, type of coverage, amount of coverage, asset insured, and estimated current value of asset insured.

An analysis of this schedule should indicate the adequacy of insurance coverage. A review of this schedule with your insurance agent is suggested.

V. <u>CONCLUSION</u>

During the brief time allotted to this subject of the basic fundamentals of bookkeeping, we have just scratched its surface. What we have tried to do is to inform you, as small-business managers, of the importance of good records. We have described the components of the important records that you must have if you are going to manage your business efficiently and profitably. In addition, we have brought to your attention some of the subsidiary records that will aid you in managing your business.

There are other records such as breakeven charts, budgets, cost accounting systems, to mention a few, which can also benefit the progressive manager. However, we do not have the time even to give you the highlights of those management tools. Your accountant can assist you in learning to understand and use them. Moreover, he can help you to develop and use the records we have discussed. For further information about them, you also can read the publications of the Small Business Administration, some of which are available to you free of charge.

By reading and using the accounting advice available to you, you can make sure that you have the right records to improve your managing skill and thereby increase your profits.

ANSWER SHEET

TEST NO. _____ PART _____ TITLE OF POSITION _____

(AS GIVEN IN EXAMINATION ANNOUNCEMENT - INCLUDE OPTION, IF ANY)

PLACE OF EXAMINATION _____ DATE _____

(CITY OR TOWN) (STATE)

RATING

USE THE SPECIAL PENCIL.   MAKE GLOSSY BLACK MARKS.

	A B C D E		A B C D E		A B C D E		A B C D E		A B C D E
1		26		51		76		101	
2		27		52		77		102	
3		28		53		78		103	
4		29		54		79		104	
5		30		55		80		105	
6		31		56		81		106	
7		32		57		82		107	
8		33		58		83		108	
9		34		59		84		109	
10		35		60		85		110	

Make only ONE mark for each answer.   Additional and stray marks may be counted as mistakes.   In making corrections, erase errors COMPLETELY.

	A B C D E		A B C D E		A B C D E		A B C D E		A B C D E
11		36		61		86		111	
12		37		62		87		112	
13		38		63		88		113	
14		39		64		89		114	
15		40		65		90		115	
16		41		66		91		116	
17		42		67		92		117	
18		43		68		93		118	
19		44		69		94		119	
20		45		70		95		120	
21		46		71		96		121	
22		47		72		97		122	
23		48		73		98		123	
24		49		74		99		124	
25		50		75		100		125	

ANSWER SHEET

TEST NO. _____ PART _____ TITLE OF POSITION _____

(AS GIVEN IN EXAMINATION ANNOUNCEMENT - INCLUDE OPTION, IF ANY)

PLACE OF EXAMINATION _____ DATE _____

(CITY OR TOWN)   (STATE)

RATING

USE THE SPECIAL PENCIL. MAKE GLOSSY BLACK MARKS.

	A B C D E		A B C D E		A B C D E		A B C D E		A B C D E
1	:: :: :: :: ::	26	:: :: :: :: ::	51	:: :: :: :: ::	76	:: :: :: :: ::	101	:: :: :: :: ::
2	:: :: :: :: ::	27	:: :: :: :: ::	52	:: :: :: :: ::	77	:: :: :: :: ::	102	:: :: :: :: ::
3	:: :: :: :: ::	28	:: :: :: :: ::	53	:: :: :: :: ::	78	:: :: :: :: ::	103	:: :: :: :: ::
4	:: :: :: :: ::	29	:: :: :: :: ::	54	:: :: :: :: ::	79	:: :: :: :: ::	104	:: :: :: :: ::
5	:: :: :: :: ::	30	:: :: :: :: ::	55	:: :: :: :: ::	80	:: :: :: :: ::	105	:: :: :: :: ::
6	:: :: :: :: ::	31	:: :: :: :: ::	56	:: :: :: :: ::	81	:: :: :: :: ::	106	:: :: :: :: ::
7	:: :: :: :: ::	32	:: :: :: :: ::	57	:: :: :: :: ::	82	:: :: :: :: ::	107	:: :: :: :: ::
8	:: :: :: :: ::	33	:: :: :: :: ::	58	:: :: :: :: ::	83	:: :: :: :: ::	108	:: :: :: :: ::
9	:: :: :: :: ::	34	:: :: :: :: ::	59	:: :: :: :: ::	84	:: :: :: :: ::	109	:: :: :: :: ::
10	:: :: :: :: ::	35	:: :: :: :: ::	60	:: :: :: :: ::	85	:: :: :: :: ::	110	:: :: :: :: ::

Make only ONE mark for each answer. Additional and stray marks may be counted as mistakes. In making corrections, erase errors COMPLETELY.

	A B C D E		A B C D E		A B C D E		A B C D E		A B C D E
11	:: :: :: :: ::	36	:: :: :: :: ::	61	:: :: :: :: ::	86	:: :: :: :: ::	111	:: :: :: :: ::
12	:: :: :: :: ::	37	:: :: :: :: ::	62	:: :: :: :: ::	87	:: :: :: :: ::	112	:: :: :: :: ::
13	:: :: :: :: ::	38	:: :: :: :: ::	63	:: :: :: :: ::	88	:: :: :: :: ::	113	:: :: :: :: ::
14	:: :: :: :: ::	39	:: :: :: :: ::	64	:: :: :: :: ::	89	:: :: :: :: ::	114	:: :: :: :: ::
15	:: :: :: :: ::	40	:: :: :: :: ::	65	:: :: :: :: ::	90	:: :: :: :: ::	115	:: :: :: :: ::
16	:: :: :: :: ::	41	:: :: :: :: ::	66	:: :: :: :: ::	91	:: :: :: :: ::	116	:: :: :: :: ::
17	:: :: :: :: ::	42	:: :: :: :: ::	67	:: :: :: :: ::	92	:: :: :: :: ::	117	:: :: :: :: ::
18	:: :: :: :: ::	43	:: :: :: :: ::	68	:: :: :: :: ::	93	:: :: :: :: ::	118	:: :: :: :: ::
19	:: :: :: :: ::	44	:: :: :: :: ::	69	:: :: :: :: ::	94	:: :: :: :: ::	119	:: :: :: :: ::
20	:: :: :: :: ::	45	:: :: :: :: ::	70	:: :: :: :: ::	95	:: :: :: :: ::	120	:: :: :: :: ::
21	:: :: :: :: ::	46	:: :: :: :: ::	71	:: :: :: :: ::	96	:: :: :: :: ::	121	:: :: :: :: ::
22	:: :: :: :: ::	47	:: :: :: :: ::	72	:: :: :: :: ::	97	:: :: :: :: ::	122	:: :: :: :: ::
23	:: :: :: :: ::	48	:: :: :: :: ::	73	:: :: :: :: ::	98	:: :: :: :: ::	123	:: :: :: :: ::
24	:: :: :: :: ::	49	:: :: :: :: ::	74	:: :: :: :: ::	99	:: :: :: :: ::	124	:: :: :: :: ::
25	:: :: :: :: ::	50	:: :: :: :: ::	75	:: :: :: :: ::	100	:: :: :: :: ::	125	:: :: :: :: ::